Business Guides on the Go

"Business Guides on the Go" presents cutting-edge insights from practice on particular topics within the fields of business, management, and finance. Written by practitioners and experts in a concise and accessible form the series provides professionals with a general understanding and a first practical approach to latest developments in business strategy, leadership, operations, HR management, innovation and technology management, marketing or digitalization. Students of business administration or management will also benefit from these practical guides for their future occupation/careers.

These Guides suit the needs of today's fast reader.

Alexander Schwarz-Musch
Alexander Tauchhammer
Bernhard Guetz

Digital Advertising in the Post-cookie Era

Strategic Campaign Planning Across the Customer Journey

Alexander Schwarz-Musch
Carinthia University of Applied Sciences
Villach, Austria

Alexander Tauchhammer
Carinthia University of Applied Sciences
Villach, Austria

Bernhard Guetz
Carinthia University of Applied Sciences
Villach, Austria

ISSN 2731-4758   ISSN 2731-4766 (electronic)
Business Guides on the Go
ISBN 978-3-658-47099-9   ISBN 978-3-658-47100-2 (eBook)
https://doi.org/10.1007/978-3-658-47100-2

Translation from the German language edition: "Digitale Werbung in der Post-Cookie-Ära" by Alexander Schwarz-Musch et al., © The Author(s)/Editor(s), exclusively licensed to Springer Fachmedien Wiesbaden GmbH, a part of Springer Nature 2024. Published by Springer Gabler Wiesbaden. All Rights Reserved.

© The Editor(s) (if applicable) and The Author(s), under exclusive license to Springer Fachmedien Wiesbaden GmbH, part of Springer Nature 2025

This work is subject to copyright. All rights are solely and exclusively licensed by the Publisher, whether the whole or part of the material is concerned, specifically the rights of translation, reprinting, reuse of illustrations, recitation, broadcasting, reproduction on microfilms or in any other physical way, and transmission or information storage and retrieval, electronic adaptation, computer software, or by similar or dissimilar methodology now known or hereafter developed.
The use of general descriptive names, registered names, trademarks, service marks, etc. in this publication does not imply, even in the absence of a specific statement, that such names are exempt from the relevant protective laws and regulations and therefore free for general use.
The publisher, the authors and the editors are safe to assume that the advice and information in this book are believed to be true and accurate at the date of publication. Neither the publisher nor the authors or the editors give a warranty, expressed or implied, with respect to the material contained herein or for any errors or omissions that may have been made. The publisher remains neutral with regard to jurisdictional claims in published maps and institutional affiliations.

This Springer imprint is published by the registered company Springer Fachmedien Wiesbaden GmbH, part of Springer Nature.
The registered company address is: Abraham-Lincoln-Str. 46, 65189 Wiesbaden, Germany

If disposing of this product, please recycle the paper.

Preface

The digital transformation has fundamentally changed the advertising industry in recent years and presented it with new challenges. In particular, the elimination of third-party cookies marks a turning point that is bringing disruptive changes to the advertising industry. In this book, we take a closer look at this decisive step and offer practical insights into the changing landscape of digital advertising. With this book, we aim to provide not only theoretical knowledge but also practical insights to help readers succeed in digital advertising in the post-cookie era.

To begin with, we provide a comprehensive overview of the campaign structure and the definition of the customer journey and campaign groups through to the planning and implementation of sub-campaigns in the various phases of the customer journey. This includes basic considerations such as clarifying the initial situation and objectives, developing buyer personas, and defining the customer journey and campaign groups through to budgeting. Another focus is on the areas of social media advertising, search engine advertising, and display advertising. Not only are the general approach and performance measurement explained but specific application options on platforms such as Facebook and Instagram, LinkedIn, YouTube, Google, and Bing are also presented. An outlook also provides an insight into the future development of these forms of advertising.

Special thanks go to all those who contributed to the creation of this book. The collaboration with the experts who shared their extensive knowledge and experience in the respective subject areas was invaluable. Our thanks also go to all those who supported and enabled the development and implementation of this project.

Villach, Austria	Alexander Schwarz-Musch
Villach, Austria	Alexander Tauchhammer
Villach, Austria	Bernhard Guetz

Contents

1 Advertising in a Digital Environment   1
  1.1 Evolution Toward the Current Status Quo   1
  1.2 Disruptive Change—The Path to the Post-cookie Era   3
    1.2.1 Third-Party Cookies: A Key Technology in Online Marketing   3
    1.2.2 The Elimination of Third-Party Cookies—Disrupting the Advertising Industry   4
    1.2.3 Evolution and Challenges of Online Targeting   7
  1.3 Current Targeting Options for Online Advertising Media to Achieve Advertising Objectives   8
    1.3.1 Contextual Targeting   8
    1.3.2 Semantic Targeting   11
    1.3.3 Predictive Targeting   12
    1.3.4 Cohort or Interest Targeting   13
    1.3.5 First-Party Data Approach   15
  References   22

2 Campaign Planning and Implementation — 27
- 2.1 Preliminary Considerations for Structuring the Campaign — 27
- 2.2 Step 1: Key Campaign Decisions — 29
  - 2.2.1 Clarifying the Starting Point and Objectives — 29
  - 2.2.2 Developing the Buyer Personas — 31
  - 2.2.3 Definition of Customer Journey and Campaign Groups — 45
  - 2.2.4 Budgeting — 51
- 2.3 Step 2: Plan and Execute the Sub-campaigns at Each Stage of the Customer Journey — 56
  - 2.3.1 Planning Basis for the Sub-campaigns — 56
  - 2.3.2 Media Planning—Channel Selection — 57
  - 2.3.3 Design of Advertising Material — 60
  - 2.3.4 Booking Advertising — 64
- 2.4 Step 3: Success Monitoring and Optimization — 68
  - 2.4.1 Performance Measurement and Optimization — 68
  - 2.4.2 Refining the Initial Buyer Persona — 78
- References — 80

3 Social Media Advertising — 85
- 3.1 Social Media in a Nutshell — 85
- 3.2 Basic Procedure — 91
- 3.3 Measuring Success on Social Media — 98
- 3.4 Application on Selected Channels — 99
  - 3.4.1 Facebook and Instagram — 100
  - 3.4.2 LinkedIn — 104
  - 3.4.3 YouTube — 109
  - 3.4.4 TikTok — 114
- 3.5 Outlook — 119
- References — 119

4	**Search Engine Advertising**	125
	4.1 SEA in a Nutshell	125
	4.2 Basic Procedure	130
	4.3 Measuring Success in the Area of Search Engine Advertising	134
	4.4 Application on Selected Search Engines	136
	4.4.1 Google	136
	4.4.2 Bing	141
	4.5 Outlook	145
	References	146
5	**Display Advertising**	149
	5.1 Characteristics of Display and Programmatic Advertising	149
	5.1.1 Ad Server as the Base Technology for Display Advertising	149
	5.1.2 Programmatic Advertising	153
	5.2 Campaign Settings	161
	5.2.1 Goals, Performance Measurement, and Optimization	161
	5.2.2 Targeting and Booking Options	162
	5.2.3 Quality Criteria	164
	References	167

About the Authors

Bernhard Guetz BA, MSc, heads the Bachelor's degree program in Digital Marketing & Sales at Carinthia University of Applied Sciences, where he teaches and conducts research in Marketing & Digital Marketing. With years of practical experience in strategic and operational marketing—especially in content marketing, promotion, and customer satisfaction management—he brings valuable industry insights into his academic work. His research focuses on customer experience, social media, review platforms, and sustainable energy use. Dr. Guetz is also an active board member of the Competence Circle Marketing, supporting the exchange of knowledge among marketing professionals. His commitment is to inspire the next generation of marketing experts and to drive sustainable advancements in the field.

Alexander Schwarz-Musch is Professor of Marketing and Market Research and leads the Master's program in Business Development & Management at Carinthia University of Applied Sciences. With a focus on business development as well as strategic and digital marketing, he brings a wealth of experience from his consulting work with national and international clients across B2B, B2C, and service sectors. He is the author of several specialist books, a lecturer in postgraduate programs, and a founding member of the Competence Circle Marketing. As the co-founder of a consulting firm, he draws on hands-on management and entrepreneurial experience, integrating practical insights into his teaching and publications to bridge academic knowledge with industry application.

Alexander Tauchhammer is a digital pioneer with over 25 years of experience in digital marketing. Since 2005, he has built and led global digital marketing efforts at Dr. Oetker, served as Digital Transformation Officer (DTO) in digital transformation projects, and now holds a leadership role at Dr. Oetker Austria. Since 2015, he has been teaching at Carinthia University of Applied Sciences, where, as a Professor of Digital Transformation, he shares his knowledge and experience with the university's students. Previously, Alexander Tauchhammer worked on both the agency and client sides in innovative and digital startups, with many of his projects earning recognition at leading digital industry awards.

1

Advertising in a Digital Environment

What You Will Take Away from This Chapter

- How digital advertising has developed into the current status quo.
- How the post-cookie era is leading to disruptive changes in the advertising industry.
- Which targeting options remain due to the elimination of third-party cookies, as well as their advantages and disadvantages.

1.1 Evolution Toward the Current Status Quo

The first banner ad ran on October 27, 1994. The North American telecommunications company AT&T paid $30,000 for a three-month banner on the website of the technology magazine Wired. The click-through rate at the time was an astounding 44%, which today—with average click-through rates of less than 1% for banner ads—would be a desirable figure (Kanarick & Timmons, 2014).

Example
- In 1995 the TKP (thousand contact price) billing was introduced.
- 1997 Pop-ups
- 1999 saw the introduction of pay-per-click billing and search engine advertising
- Google launched AdWords in 2000 (Reed, n.d.)

In 2000, however, there were already advanced technologies such as ad servers with profiling, advertising on cell phones (via SMS), video advertising, advertising opportunities on enhanced TV (now smart TV), etc. The technologies are still very similar today, but at that time the bandwidths were too low and the number of Internet users was still very small. This should change dramatically in the next 20 years.

Today, digital advertising accounts for the majority of global advertising spending. According to IAB-Europe, around 92 billion euros were spent on digital advertising in Europe alone in 2021. The UK leads the way with EUR 32.334 billion, followed by Germany (EUR 12.144 billion) and France (EUR 8.360 billion) (IAB Europe, 2022). Depending on the client and the method of measurement, the data collected on the distribution of ad spending may differ by a few percentage points—but not in the order of the top 2 advertising media: here, digital media is in first place and TV in second place. According to Dentsu, one of the world's largest agencies, digital media accounted for approximately 52.8% of global ad spending in 2022, followed by TV in second place at 27.4% with further growth forecast for both channels. Print, out-of-home, radio, and cinema advertising are following in the single-digit percentages (Dentsu, 2022).

This reflects the significant changes in media consumption patterns brought about by the Internet and smartphones. However, it would be wrong to say that "traditional media" are dying out; rather, a process of change is underway that is blurring the lines between digital and analog media: Digital and TV are merging into smart TV, digital and radio into Live Radio. Last but not least, the combination of traditional and digital media in the media mix can lead to increased efficiency, which underlines the relevance and importance of traditional media.

However, there are disruptive changes that are shaking up this multi-billion-dollar market worldwide.

1.2 Disruptive Change—The Path to the Post-cookie Era

1.2.1 Third-Party Cookies: A Key Technology in Online Marketing

In the online world, users often encounter content, such as banner ads or videos, that is not directly from the website they are visiting, but embedded from another provider. When a user visits a website, the browser loads content not only from that specific website, but also from these other providers. These external providers may store cookies on the user's device when loading their content. Since these cookies do not come directly from the website visited, but from a third party, they are called third party cookies. They make it possible to track the user's behavior across different websites.

Unlike first-party cookies, which come directly from the website you visit, third-party cookies are stored on the server of the advertising provider. This server creates user profiles that can then be targeted with appropriate advertising. The following example illustrates how third-party cookies work.

Example Have you ever had the experience of being "stalked" by an ad? For example, you read a travel article about Rome on the Internet. A few hours or days later, you also read the latest news on the Internet and see ads for flights to Rome and hotels in the Italian capital as banner ads. If you then go to the airline's website to check the prices for flights to Rome but don't book them, you might even see a voucher for a flight to Rome the next day in a banner ad.

Technically, this is all made possible by third-party cookies; the advertising technology behind it is known as "retargeting." Retargeting makes it possible to respond to customer needs and issues at every stage of the customer journey, increasing advertising efficiency. Sometimes, however, advertising systems are not set up very intelligently, so you may still see the airline's ad on the airline's website weeks after you booked your flight.

This example shows how third-party cookies basically work. They collect information about the behavior of Internet users, such as shopping habits or websites visited. This data is stored anonymously and can even be tracked from one website to the next. This technique is very effective in online marketing. It helps to select users for special advertising campaigns. It can also be used to create audiences that can be targeted on major advertising platforms such as Google and Facebook.

In addition, cookies can be used to show ads that are relevant to the user's financial situation.

Example Users browse a real estate website and search for high-priced listings. They then search for kitchens on the Internet and are shown advertisements from a furniture store with kitchens in the upper price range. This also works the other way around, using the example of students searching for an affordable rental apartment on the same real estate site. In the same search for kitchen furniture on the Internet, they will be shown ads for a low-cost kitchen.

Another option enabled by third-party cookies is lookalike modeling. This looks for cookie profile twins of your own customers in the ad networks. The assumption is that people with the same cookie profile will be interested in similar ads. Another important advantage of third-party cookies is that they can be used to measure and optimize advertising campaigns in real time, increasing the efficiency of advertising during the campaign rather than only after the campaign has ended.

1.2.2 The Elimination of Third-Party Cookies— Disrupting the Advertising Industry

This approach to data collection has repeatedly drawn criticism from privacy advocates, and legislation has worked to improve privacy over the years. Since 2002, the e-Privacy Directive has regulated the minimum requirements for data protection in the telecommunications sector and aims to protect the fundamental rights and privacy of EU citizens. It was last amended in 2009 to limit the information that can be stored on users' devices. Essentially, users should be clearly informed about the collection and processing of data, and should be able to opt in or out. The EU has one of the strictest cookie policies (Husain, 2023).

> **Legal**
> Member States shall ensure that the storing of information, or the gaining of access to information already stored, in the terminal equipment of a subscriber or user is only allowed on condition that the subscriber or user concerned has given his or her consent, having been provided with clear and comprehensive information, in accordance with Directive 95/46/EC, inter alia, about the purposes of the processing. This shall not prevent any technical storage or access for the sole purpose of carrying out the transmission of a communication over an electronic communications network, or as strictly necessary in order for the provider of an information society service explicitly requested by the subscriber or user to provide the service. (European Parliament and Council of the European Union, 2002, Art. 5, Abs. 3, Directive 2002/58/EC)

However, the e-Privacy Directive should not be confused with the e-Privacy Regulation, which the EU has been drafting since 2017, as EU member states have not yet been able to agree on a final legal text (as of August 2024). The e-Privacy Regulation regulates electronic communications and data protection, and will replace the General Data Protection Regulation (GDPR) and the e-Privacy Directive in the near future. The applicability of the e-Privacy Regulation will therefore not start before 2025, after the end of the transition period (CMS, 2020).

In other countries, such as the UK, China, Brazil, Egypt, and South Africa, users must also give their consent (cookie consent) when personal data is collected, although in Australia and New Zealand "only" information is required to a lesser extent. In the USA, there is no uniform federal cookie law, i.e., cookie consent is required by law. However, some states (California, Virginia, Connecticut) have their own laws that provide for consent, opt-out, or other notice requirements. Canada's privacy laws are stricter than those in the USA and regulate the use of cookies through anti-spam and privacy laws (Husain, 2023; Laird, 2023).

All of these regulatory tightening around the world have led major browser providers such as Apple's Safari and Mozilla's Firefox to shorten cookie lifespans or block third-party cookies. With Safari, Apple became the second browser vendor to block all third-party cookies in 2020, and users can accept or block tracking from websites, third parties, and advertisers at any time. In this way, Apple aims to prevent cross-site tracking and make web browsing safer (Bohn, 2020; Apple, 2024). The introduction of ATT has led to significantly lower user tracking rates, with less than half of users consenting to tracking, although there are big differences between industries and countries. The gaming industry has the highest ATT opt-in rates at 39%, while education apps have the lowest rates. The United Arab Emirates has the highest opt-in rate at almost 50%, while Germany has the lowest rate at 20%. It is clear that Apple's ATT framework has significantly changed the advertising landscape and has also had a massive impact on large advertising networks such as Google, Facebook, and Snapchat, which are struggling to track users and serve personalized ads. The lower tracking rates are forcing advertisers to adapt and find new ways to reach users (Curry, 2024).

How high the proportion of third-party cookies will ultimately be also depends heavily on Google, which has a global market share of 65% with its Chrome browser (StatCounter, 2024). In fact, Google has already announced several times that it will eliminate third-party cookies with its Chrome browser. However, the announced dates have been repeatedly postponed and finally the announced discontinuation has been reversed. This means that Google will not automatically disable third-party cookies, but will leave the decision about the use of third-party data cookies to the user in a transparent manner (Chavez, 2024). This will undoubtedly increase the opt-out rate. No one can yet predict how high (Sluis, 2024).

In summary, such a sharp decline in third-party cookies will lead to a radical change in the advertising industry, making a rethink imperative.

1.2.3 Evolution and Challenges of Online Targeting

As early as 2000, there were leading ad server technologies based on cookies that could build user profiles and programmatically serve and optimize ads in real time across websites and smart TVs (then called enhanced TVs).

However, advertising using third-party cookies or these new technologies was not always the best solution. This is because user profiles are created based on browsing behavior, but a user profile is not a single person, but the client, i.e., a mobile phone, tablet, smart TV, etc. These can also be used by multiple people. These can also be used by multiple people, so the user profile created is a sum of multiple people. In addition, a person's browsing behavior cannot be measured across clients without logging in. As a result, it is not possible to create an accurate user profile of an individual using third-party cookies.

Cross-site tracking has been a key technology in recent years, but will no longer be applicable in current systems due to the disappearance of third-party cookies. This technology used cookies to track a user's online behavior across different websites. Without these cookies, comprehensive retargeting across multiple ad networks is no longer possible, severely limiting the ability to search for specific user profiles in the context of advertising.

The cookie-less era will therefore require new technological solutions to these problems, which are already being worked on. However, it is also important that "old" (already known) targeting options are used or combined with new technological solutions. We will look at what these are at the moment in the next chapter.

1.3 Current Targeting Options for Online Advertising Media to Achieve Advertising Objectives

Since the introduction of advertising in digital media, targeting has been possible without third-party cookies. The approaches used for targeting can still be used successfully today. In some cases, campaigns based on targeting can be more efficient than those based on user profiles. In the cookie-free era, advertisers have access to the following targeting options, which can be used individually or in combination.

- Contextual targeting.
- Semantic targeting.
- Predictive targeting.
- Cohort or interest targeting.
- First-party data approach.

1.3.1 Contextual Targeting

Contextual targeting is probably as old as the advertising industry itself. This is because the advertising industry quickly discovered that placing advertising in an affine environment increases turnover and sales. Contextual advertising (CA) is an advertising method in which ads are placed in a media context relevant to the content in order to optimize the effectiveness of the advertising. CA analyzes the content of a website or app to understand the context. This context can include topics, keywords, sentiment, and other relevant factors. Based on this context, ads that are relevant to the respective context are selected and displayed to the user (Häglund & Björklund, 2024). Contextual targeting and contextual advertising are closely related concepts. Contextual targeting is the method or strategy for selecting relevant ads, while contextual advertising is the result of this process—the ads that are presented to the user.

Contextual targeting is probably as old as the advertising industry itself. In fact, the advertising industry was quick to discover that placing ads in an affine environment increases revenue and sales. Simply put, if you want to sell tennis shoes, they are best placed on the sports pages of a daily newspaper or in a sports magazine—especially in the tennis section. A second simple method is digital keyword targeting. For example, select the keyword "tennis shoe" or "tennis" and the ad will appear in all digital newspaper articles where these words appear. From a broader perspective, Google keyword advertising can also be classified as contextual targeting.

Contextual targeting can also completely miss the advertising target if words that sound the same have different meanings. For example, recipes can be cooking recipes or drug prescriptions, which are completely different in content. But the environment also needs to be considered. A food company had booked a defibrillator as a product ad on a reputable newspaper website using the keyword "cardiac arrest." Unfortunately, there were several deaths at a mountain running event in Germany due to bad weather, sub-zero temperatures, and subsequent cardiac arrests. The product "defibrillator" is a perfect match for "cardiac arrest," but the ad in the context of the tragic mountain running event was rated very negatively by readers. In such cases, contextual targeting can be used with a "black list," i.e., such cases can be excluded from ad bookings. You can also use this to prevent your ads from being served in conjunction with articles with problematic content (e.g., murder, terrorism, sexual content). These issues are collectively referred to as "brand safety." These are practices and tools that display ads only in positive environments/contexts.

However, with contextual targeting, many media face an inventory problem: if too many advertisers want to be in the same ad environment at the same time, advertisers will not have enough ad space (inventory) to sell. Third-party cookies could be used, for example, to reach users interested in tennis on other sites or subsites where advertising inventory is still available. This is because a user profile is usually not only interested in tennis, but also in other areas of interest, such as cars, cooking, or travel, based on their browsing behavior. In this case, you may find that users interested in tennis can be reached there if the ad inventory on the tennis sites is fully booked.

However, with the elimination of third-party cookies, this will no longer be as easy. However, there is an opportunity to work with first-party data, where the company itself has requested information about the areas of interest of your tennis shoe buyers. For more details, see the other approaches under first-party data.

Contextual Targeting Combined with the Customer Journey

Media sites or content providers such as news portals, online magazines, or specialized blogs and websites offer another opportunity to reach audiences through contextual targeting. Similar to print media, these sites offer high-quality content ranging from general content (e.g., the online pages of daily newspapers) to niche content (e.g., sites dedicated to specific topics such as watches or hobbies such as fly fishing). Waste can be minimized, especially on sites that cover niche topics that are of interest to your target audience. At the same time, higher costs and therefore "worse" CPMs, CPCs, or CPSs must be accepted due to the generally lower reach.

Example Sports company with e-bikes (see Fig. 1.1): The goal of the campaign was to raise awareness about e-bikes. The campaign aimed to show that e-bikes are suitable for everyone. "It doesn't matter if you are an athlete or not—or if you have a high or low budget. E-bike specialist XXXL Sports has the right products for you."

The implementation was as follows: a teaser article about e-bikes was placed on the home page or sub-pages of various media. When users clicked on the headline of the e-bike article, they were taken to the detailed article page where 5 inspiring reasons were given as to why now is the right time to buy an e-bike. The reasons included rising fuel prices, being able to ride even if you're not in the best shape, having to worry about transportation, and the fact that e-bikes are available in all price ranges. XXXL Sports was deliberately not named as the source of the article in order to increase the credibility of the article. However, ads for XXXL Sports' expert tips and e-bike offers in the online store were placed around the article.

Potential customers were thus guided through the entire customer journey: from a teaser in the inspiration phase, to the detailed article in

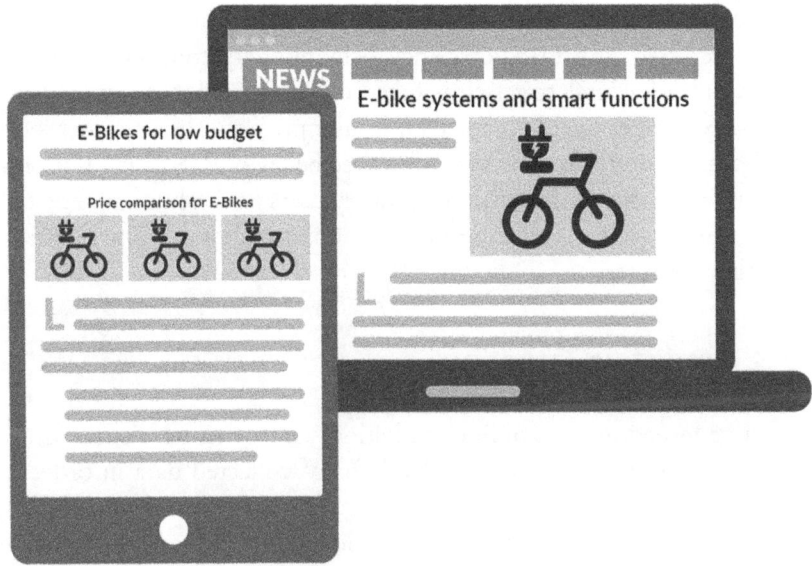

Fig. 1.1 Example sports company

the information search phase, to the expert tips in the purchase decision phase, to the e-bike offer in the online store in the purchase phase.

From the point of view of XXXL Sports, this has the advantage that almost only users who are also interested in the topic of e-bikes end up on the shop/expert tips page (Content Garden, n.d.).

Contextual targeting is becoming increasingly intelligent with the help of artificial intelligence. This means that not only text can be recognized, but also all common media genres such as images, videos, sounds, etc. This leads to an evolution from contextual targeting to semantic targeting.

1.3.2 Semantic Targeting

Semantic targeting analyzes the context of content on websites and thus sees the current situation as a whole (Crystal, 2010). This enables Google, Facebook, advertising sites (via ad servers), etc. to recognize a positive or negative environment on the medium and thus target the advertising. This increases the relevance of advertising from the user's point of view and can lead to increased advertising efficiency. Semantic targeting is done in real time, while behavioral targeting is based on the past, for example, using third-party cookies to collect behavior in user profiles. The customer journey also plays a critical role. This is because behavioral targeting not only tells you what stage of the customer journey users are in, but semantic targeting is more likely to reach users at the moment in the customer journey when they are interested in the topic (Otterbach, 2022).

1.3.3 Predictive Targeting

Predictive targeting is an online marketing strategy in which the future behavior of users is predicted on the basis of collected data in order to show them the most relevant advertising possible. Instead of targeting users based on demographic characteristics or past behavior, predictive targeting uses algorithms and machine learning to identify patterns in large data sets. These patterns make it possible to calculate probabilities for certain user actions, such as buying a certain product or visiting a certain website. This allows advertisers to make their campaigns more efficient and minimize wastage by presenting advertising to the users who are most likely to respond to it (Product et al., 2023).

Example An e-bike supplier has noticed the following behavior in its online store:

The data collected so far (e.g., product pages visited, purchases, ad clicks, location, device type, etc.) has shown that users who have purchased an e-bike in the past and visit the store's blog at least three times a week are also very likely to be interested in touring backpacks.

With this information, the online store can now target advertising for touring backpacks to this specific group of users through display advertising, personalized email marketing campaigns, or social media ads.

Predictive targeting uses the insights from data analysis to optimize marketing efforts and deliver more relevant advertising to the end user.

By eliminating third-party cookie data, large ad networks are attempting to analyze historical data, enrich it with additional first- and third-party data, and thus predict an assessment of behavior independent of the user. Predictive targeting can also be seen as an evolution of semantic targeting and can be used regardless of the context of a website or TV program. Age, buying behavior, etc., can also be estimated by the predictive algorithm, which can be used to enrich user profiles or personas.

The better the quality of the data collected and the predictive algorithm, the more accurate the predictions and the more effective the advertising. This predictive algorithm often uses artificial intelligence. For example, if someone is buying large quantities of laundry detergent online, the algorithm may infer that it is a large family, especially if the orders are more frequent than for other customers. This customer group may not want to carry heavy packages of detergent all the time, so they order online. Based on the order data, an online retailer might predict that these customers will search for or purchase laundry detergent every three weeks. If retailers have the customer's email address, they could send targeted offers such as "Buy 2 packs and get 1 free" (Dastani Consulting, 2022).

Predictive targeting can also be used for future advertising via ad servers on websites, smart TVs, digital radio, digital outdoor advertising (TV screens in subways), etc.

Example A beer company recently bought a number of smaller breweries that are very popular in their regions, but less well-known nationally. Therefore, it makes the most sense to advertise regionally. In addition, sales figures show that more beer is consumed when it is at least 20 degrees outside. Weather and location data is used in the AdServer to serve ads. This ensures that the ads for the appropriate regional beer brand are delivered exactly where it is currently warmer than 20 degrees.

1.3.4 Cohort or Interest Targeting

The fundamental problem with third-party cookies is that users can be "identified" and inferences can be made about an individual. Although third-party cookies are stored anonymously, the EU and privacy experts have shown that this can easily be circumvented by targeted data collection. The purpose of the EU Privacy Regulation is to prevent this by eliminating third-party cookies.

Browser providers, such as Google with Google Chrome, see this as an opportunity for targeted advertising for the time after the GDPR is implemented into European and national law. This is because Google can measure browsing behavior through Google Chrome and thus analyze the behavior and performance of groups of users, rather than individual users, who share common characteristics. These groups of users are called cohorts (Google, 2023).

However, cohorts can only be used effectively if a very large database is available. With Google Chrome, Google has over 60% market share of browsers used for Internet use. It is followed by Edge, Firefox, and Safari with around 10%. This could further increase Google's market power in the advertising industry (StatCounter, 2023).

However, cohort targeting is also controversial from a privacy perspective. This is because the selection of cohorts can be narrowed down to the point where it is possible to assign them to individual users. For this reason, Google will discontinue its FLOC (Federal Learning of Cohorts) program, which uses numeric IDs, in 2022 and replace it with topic-based IDs. Analyzing browsing history allows to determine the interests of users by recording what types of websites are visited. This information is used to provide targeted and relevant advertising. Importantly, interests are determined locally in the browser and no data is sent to Google or other third parties. Instead, the data is processed on the user's device and categorized into "themes" that reflect the user's interests. These themes are associated with the websites that a user frequently visits. To protect privacy, the interests calculated in this way are deleted periodically, although with the Topics API this happens monthly (Google, n.d.; Abrams, 2023 September 9).

Other companies, such as Adobe, continue to offer cohort analysis for use in advertising campaigns. From an advertiser's perspective, the question is whether cohort targeting or topic-based targeting is an efficient targeting option, or whether other targeting options are more efficient depending on the campaign objective (Adobe, 2023).

1.3.5 First-Party Data Approach

1.3.5.1 Key Questions for a First-Party Data Approach

The concept of first-party data is as old as marketing itself. Think back to the days when small grocery companies knew their customers by name and knew exactly what they bought and when. This traditional principle has been applied to digital marketing. Especially in an era without cookies, first-party data is becoming more important again. The reasons are obvious: users share this data voluntarily, it offers direct contact options such as email or phone, and it signals an interest in the products and services offered (Wagner, 2022).

But is first-party data the answer to a cookie-less future? Simply collecting data such as name, address, and date of birth will not necessarily improve advertising effectiveness. Before you start collecting data, you should have a solid first-party data strategy in place. The central question should be: "What data can I use to drive sales, and how does advertising effectiveness compare to other traditional and digital advertising options?" Ultimately, the measurement of advertising effectiveness (ROI) also plays a key role. Sometimes contextual targeting may simply be more efficient than an extensive and expensive first-party data approach. Often, however, a combination of the two is most effective. Therefore, it is essential to constantly monitor ROI, sales, and other KPIs that are important to you across all marketing and advertising efforts.

But how do you build a first-party data approach? Figure 1.2 provides an overview of the components of a typical first-party data concept. On the right-hand side of the figure are the advertising, analysis, and marketing areas, where all first-party data actions are carried out toward the user: new data is then collected in the user profile database (CDP Consumer Data Platform).

The left side is very important at the beginning of a first-party concept, because you first have to get the active consent of the users: at the touchpoints (consent management) in order to collect data. Identity management is the technical core in between, how users can be identified over time in a technically and legally compliant way, so that, for example,

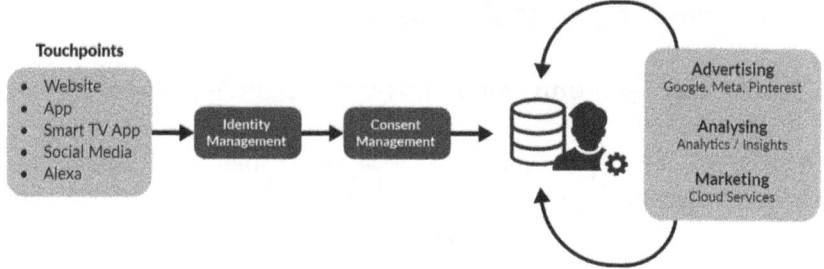

Fig. 1.2 First-party data approach

personalized advertising can be displayed based on the user profile. More details and examples will follow in the next sections.

A first-party data approach must answer the following questions:

"How do I use which data in advertising campaigns to generate more revenue/sales, and how does advertising efficiency compare to other advertising options?"

To answer this complex question, the first step is to develop examples of how the first-party data concept can be used to increase sales. These can be found in the Advertising, Analytics, and Marketing section on the right side of the illustration. Specific examples might include.

Example Examples of first-party data approaches that can lead to more sales/revenue with the best ROI:

- You can better understand buying behavior and improve products or promotions (Analytics area).
- You can create personalized ads or target users similar to your first-party data users in other ad networks via data clean rooms or unique identifiers (Advertising—see next paragraph).
- You can use first-party data to automate processes, such as creating automat newsletters about areas of interest from the first-party data profile and sending them individually at the right pre-purchase time (Marketing).

and much more.

Once the promising examples have been formulated, we need to look at the technical infrastructure. At the heart of first-party data approach is the Consumer Data Platform (CDP), which serves as a single source of truth for processing and managing all first-party data and future data in a central customer database.

First-party data such as name, address, date of birth, etc., is fed into the CDP. This is then combined with website usage, customer service, online and offline store activity, social media channels, etc., from all offline and online touchpoints.

The advantage of this is that you own the CDP as a company and therefore have all marketing activities in your own hands. The CDP enables everyone involved in the buying process to and derive marketing and sales activities from it.

The next question must be:

"What data do I need to successfully execute my marketing plan?"

General information about customers, such as name, date of birth, and address, is not enough to plan effective marketing and advertising campaigns. Depending on the specific objectives of the campaign, it is necessary to determine which customer data is required to successfully implement the concepts. For example, specific information on purchasing behavior, shopping basket size, media usage, needs, specific pain points, etc. A company should ask these questions not only when creating a first-party data concept, but as an ongoing process after every marketing and advertising activity. This is because measuring success can lead to further conclusions and identify white spots in the customer profile. These can be closed by collecting additional relevant customer data during subsequent data collection activities.

The last and first question in our cycle is:

"How do I get the data and how do I get users to give me their data voluntarily and correctly?"

The answer is simple: there must be **relevant** value for users. To date, attempts have been made to collect data from users through contests.

However, this approach often falls short because users often do not provide accurate information about their age, hobbies, etc. For this reason, it is crucial for companies to find smarter ways to collect correct data from users with a higher probability. Value-added measures such as birthday vouchers for the online store, customer clubs or special communities such as product tester communities are starting points.

Consent management is especially important. From a legal perspective, a company must first obtain the user's informed consent to the disclosure of data in accordance with data protection regulations. In most cases, this is done with the help of a consent management tool. This is because companies must be able to prove that they have obtained users' consent. One way to do this is to have a consent form on a website where users agree to the terms of tracking or other activities. However, this must be done actively; circumvention through implicit consent by clicking or scrolling must no longer be used. It must also provide accurate information about what data is being collected and for what purpose. Users must also be able to withdraw their consent as easily as they gave it. The "opt-in" button must be the same size as the "opt-out" button, and if there are checkboxes, they must not be pre-populated (noyb – European Center for Digital Rights, 2023).

All of these "tricks" were popular in the past to make consent forms look better. However, this has changed as fines can be as high as 4% of a company's annual turnover (European Data Protection Authority, 2022).

Example A large TV network uses digitization to offer successful TV content on demand and live for free in a country (local content). To gain access, users simply to download the app and register. They can then watch the TV content on demand or even live on their smartphone, tablet, or TV screen (mirrored on smart TV).

Media consumption patterns and programs are stored in the user profile. In addition, data from third-party market research companies is integrated and the user profile is continuously expanded. Since users are always logged in, relevant advertising can be displayed based on the user profile. In fact, advertisements can be precisely tailored to the user's profile in real time.

1.3.5.2 The Role of Identity Management

Identity management is a central part of the first-party data concept and aims to ensure that users can be recognized at any time and at any touchpoint, thus building a unique user profile over time. From a technical point of view, this can be implemented in different ways, e.g., through a combination of login, email address, DMP ID, etc.

There are several privacy-compliant applications for the user profiles that are created, but they differ significantly in terms of the reach that can be achieved (see Fig. 1.3).

The advantages and disadvantages of each option can be summarized as follows:

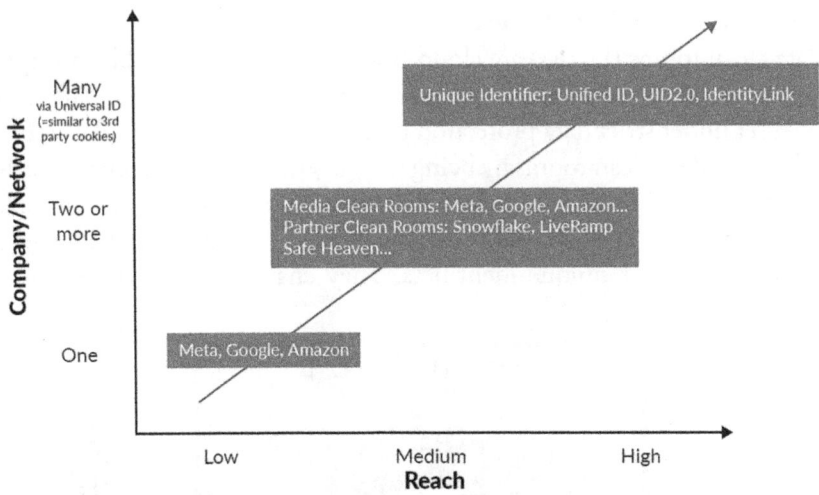

Fig. 1.3 Possible applications in identity management

1. **Use on own touchpoints or a network (e.g., Meta, Google, Amazon, etc.) = low reach.**

   First-party data concepts are perfectly possible on your own touchpoints or in a network in compliance with the EU Data Protection Regulation. However, the more you use targeting to narrow your audience, the more you will run into reach limitations.

2. **Use across multiple networks = medium range.**

   If you want to perform cross-network marketing and advertising activities, you can exchange data using data clean rooms (DCRs). Because of the cookieless time and the end of third-party cookies, data clean rooms (see Fig. 1.4) can be used to continue to target audiences with personalized advertising, gain customer insights, and measure the success of marketing activities. Of course, it is important to comply with data protection regulations and to protect users' privacy (Herbrich, 2022).

Excursus: Data Clean Rooms
Data clean rooms (DCRs) are cloud-based solutions that enable multiple parties, such as advertisers and publishers, to analyze their data sets together under strict data protection guidelines. Universal IDs play a central role in data clean rooms by being used as encrypted and secure identifiers that can link different data sets without revealing personal data. These universal IDs can take various forms, including hashed email addresses or other unique identifiers. They enable the identification of

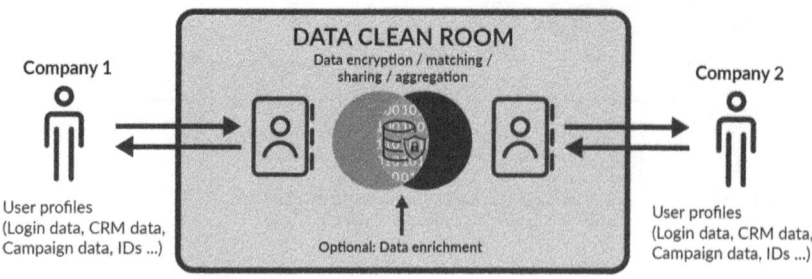

Fig. 1.4 Data clean rooms

users or entities across different data sets without revealing sensitive information. The results of data analysis in DCRs are provided in aggregated form, e.g., as cohorts or reports. This prevents the traceability of individual users and ensures data protection compliance (Databricks, n.d.; Sweeney & Figas, 2024).

There are currently the following types of DCRs:

- **Media Clean Rooms.**
  in this group are walled garden companies like Google, Meta, and Amazon or
- **Partner Clean Rooms.**
  where a company can enter into individual collaborations with other companies (Examples: Snowflake, LiveRamp Safe Haven) (Johnson, 2022).

Google uses data clean rooms through the Google Ads Data Hub product. Since discontinuing FLOC (cohort targeting), Google has relied on PAIR (Publisher Advertiser Identity Reconciliation). Advertisers and publishers can use PAIR to show ads to shared customers. First-party data is reconciled multiple times in encrypted form in clean rooms (Google Cloud, n.d.).

Amazon Marketing Cloud is used by Amazon, which also aggregates data from Wholefoods and Twitch consumer data.

Disney has built a data cleanroom based on Snowflake, Habu, and Infosum that gives advertisers access to over 1000 first-party data segments.

The AppsFlyer Privacy Cloud is the largest independent data cleanroom with interfaces to major data networks including Facebook, Google, Twitter, and Snap (Johnson, 2022).

3. **Use on many networks (Universal ID) = high range.**

An extension to many networks leads us to the topic of universal ID, since the Wallet Garden Clean Room concepts are reserved for the large reach providers such as Google, Amazon, Meta, etc., and these work with different identifiers.

In return, a small network can join the universal ID initiative to become part of a large reach network. Companies or ad networks should collect first-party data and then synchronize it with a universal and unique identifier across all publishers. This identifier can be stored in the user's browser using first-party cookies or persistent IDs (across devices). If cookie blockers are used, identification via cookies will not work either (Leino, 2021; Davies, 2017).

If this vision is realized with a universal ID provider, the current practice of marketing and advertising with third-party cookies would be almost identical. However, there are currently numerous universal ID providers on the market, such as Unified ID, UID2.0, ID5, IdentityLink, Publisher Common ID (PubCID), SharedID, Advertising ID Consortium, and many more (Insticator, 2022).

There is great interest from the advertising industry in universal identifiers so that one industry standard (e.g., ID5) can be used in the future, rather than many. Regardless of which vendor prevails, this can be implemented (Kumar et al., n.d.; ID5, n.d.; Publift, 2023).

However, all of these targeting options have pros and cons, are somewhat rigid, and often cover only one advertising objective. To make campaigns more efficient, we have developed a campaign planning process that combines personas and customer journeys with the targeting options mentioned above. We also look at how to use personas and customer journeys in strategic campaign planning, and show specific operational applications using the world's most popular digital advertising media in social media, search, and display.

References

Abrams, L. (2023, September 9). *Google rolls out privacy sandbox to use Chrome browsing history for ads*. BleepingComputer. https://www.bleepingcomputer.com/news/google/google-rolls-out-privacy-sandbox-to-use-chrome-browsing-history-for-ads/

Adobe. (2023). *Learn about cohort analysis in Adobe Analytics*. https://experienceleague.adobe.com/de/docs/analytics/analyze/analysis-workspace/visualizations/cohort-table/cohort-analysis

Apple. (2024). *Allow cookies in Safari on the Mac.* https://support.apple.com/de-at/guide/safari/ibrw850f6c51/mac
Bohn, D. (2020, March 24). *Apple's Safari now blocks all third-party cookies by default.* The Verge. https://www.theverge.com/2020/3/24/21192830/apple-safari-intelligent-tracking-privacy-full-third-party-cookie-blocking
Chavez, A. (2024, July 22). *A new path for Privacy Sandbox on the web.* Privacy Sandbox. https://privacysandbox.com/news/privacy-sandbox-update/
CMS. (2020). *E-Privacy.* https://cms.law/de/aut/insight/e-privacy
Content Garden. (n.d.). *XXL Sports & Outdoor informative expert listicle.* https://content-garden.com/project/xxlsports
Crystal, D. (2010). Semantic targeting: Past, present, and future. *ASLIB Proceedings, 62*(4/5), 355–365.
Curry, D. (2024, May 22). App *tracking transparency opt-in rates.* Business of Apps. https://www.businessofapps.com/data/att-opt-in-rates/
DASTANI Consulting. (2022). *AI vs. predictive analytics.* https://dastani.de/predictive-analytics-vs-kuenstliche-intelligenz-ki
Databricks. (n.d.). *Data clean rooms: Leverage secure data collaboration to maximize insights and performance.* Databricks. https://www.databricks.com/discover/enterprise-data-platform/clean-room
Davies, J. (2017). *WTF is a persistent ID?* Digiday. https://digiday.com/marketing/wtf-persistent-id/
Dentsu. (2022). *Dentsu ad spend report predicts continued growth through 2022 despite global economic turbulence.* https://www.dentsu.com/news-releases/dentsu-ad-spend-forecast-july-2022-release
Directive 2002/58/EC of the European Parliament and of the Council of July 12, 2002, concerning the processing of personal data and the protection of privacy in the electronic communications sector (Directive on privacy and electronic communications). (2002). Official Journal of the European Communities.
European Data Protection Board. (2022). *Guidelines 04/22 on the calculation of administrative fines under the GDPR.* https://edpb.europa.eu/system/files/2022-05/edpb_guidelines_042022_calculationofadministrativefines_en.pdf
European Parliament and Council of the European Union. (2002). Directive 2002/58/EC of the European Parliament and of the Council of 12 July 2002 concerning the processing of personal data and the protection of privacy in the electronic communications sector (Directive on privacy and electronic

communications). EUR-Lex. https://eur-lex.europa.eu/legal-content/EN/ALL/?uri=celex%3A32002L0058

Google. (2022). *Das ist die neue Topics API im Rahmen von Privacy Sandbox*. https://blog.google/intl/de-de/produkte/android-chrome-mehr/topics-api-im-privacy-sandbox/

Google. (2023). *Cohorts*. https://support.google.com/analytics/answer/6158745?hl=de#zippy=%2Cthemen-in-diesem-artikel

Google. (n.d.). *Get to know the new topics API for Privacy Sandbox*. Google Developers. https://developers.google.com/privacy-sandbox/private-advertising/topics

Google Cloud. (n.d.). *Share sensitive data with data clean rooms*. Google Cloud. https://cloud.google.com/bigquery/docs/data-clean-rooms

Häglund, E., & Björklund, J. (2024). AI-driven contextual advertising: Toward relevant messaging without personal data. *Journal of Current Issues & Research in Advertising, 45*(3), 301–319. https://doi.org/10.1080/10641734.2024.2334939

Herbrich, T. (2022). Data clean rooms. *Computer Law Review International, 23*(4), 109–120. https://doi.org/10.9785/cri-2022-230404

Husain, O. (2023). *Cookie banner requirements: GDPR, CCPA, CPRA, UK & more*. Enzuzo. https://www.enzuzo.com/blog/cookie-banner-requirements

IAB Europe. (2022). *IAB Europe releases full 2021 AdEx benchmark report to reveal digital advertising market size*. https://iabeurope.eu/knowledge-hub/iab-europe-adex-benchmark-2021-report/

ID5. (n.d.). *Future-proofed identification for digital advertising*. https://id5.io/

Insticator. (2022). *Universal IDs for publishers: A guide for non-techies*. https://www.insticator.com/universal-ids-for-publishers-a-guide-for-non-techies/

Johnson, T. (2022). *The ultimate list of data clean room providers*. Tinuiti. https://tinuiti.com/blog/data-privacy/list-of-data-clean-room-providers/

Kanarick, C., & Timmons, O. (2014). *The first banner ad*. http://thefirstbannerad.com/attmap.html

Kumar, A., O'Rourke, E., Lacuna, P., Sasane, S., Simpson, T., Jaquet, V., & King, Z. (n.d.). *What are universal IDs and why should we care?* IAB SEA+India. https://www.iabseaindia.com/blog/universal-id

Laird, J. (2023). *Cookie consent outside of the EU*. PrivacyPolicies. https://www.privacypolicies.com/blog/cookie-consent-outside-eu/

Leino, S. (2021). *How does Universal ID work when third-party cookies are going to be history?* Relevant Digital. https://blog.relevant-digital.com/how-does-universal-id-work-when-third-party-cookies-are-going-to-be-history noyb – European Center for Digital Rights. (2023). *Consent banner report: Overview of EU and national guidelines on dark patterns*. https://noyb.eu/sites/default/files/2024-07/noyb_Cookie_Report_2024.pdf

Otterbach, B. (2022). *Cookieless: Alternativen zum tracking über third party cookies*. https://onlinemarketing.de/performance-marketing/alternativen-zum-cookielosen-tracking

Product, A. A., MiQ, A., & Kumar, S. (2023). *Cookie-less predictive targeting in programmatic media using topic modelling*. In 2023 IEEE 4th international conference on pattern recognition and machine learning (PRML) (pp. 571–576).

Publift. (2023). *What is Universal ID and how can it help publishers*. https://www.publift.com/blog/what-is-universal-id-and-how-can-it-help-publishers

Reed, D. (n.d.). *History of online advertising*. Study.com. https://study.com/academy/lesson/history-of-online-advertising.html

Sluis, S. (2024). *The looming question of cookie consent*. AdExchanger. https://www.adexchanger.com/the-big-story/the-looming-question-of-cookie-consent/

StatCounter. (2023). *Desktop browser market share in Europe*. StatCounter Global Stats. https://gs.statcounter.com/browser-market-share/desktop/europe/#monthly-202407-202407-bar

StatCounter. (2024, August). *Browser market share worldwide – August 2024*. StatCounter Global Stats. https://gs.statcounter.com/browser-market-share

Sweeney, M., & Figas, N. (2024, July 30). *What is a data clean room and how does it work?* Clearcode. https://clearcode.cc/blog/data-clean-room/

Wagner, B. (2022). *First-party data improves the customer experience – if e-commerce companies use it effectively*. Salesforce. https://www.salesforce.com/de/blog/2022/10/first-party-data.html

2

Campaign Planning and Implementation

What You Will Take Away from This Chapter

- How companies can plan, execute, and monitor the success of online advertising campaigns.
- The role of campaign groups and how to develop them based on the customer journey.
- How buyer personas support the planning of online advertising campaigns and how a minimum viable persona can be created.
- What metrics can be used to measure the success of advertising at each stage of the customer journey and the role of top KPIs.

2.1 Preliminary Considerations for Structuring the Campaign

When planning online advertising campaigns, advertisers are faced with a very fundamental question:

Question How do we ensure that our advertising efforts are successful and help us achieve our sales goals?

This challenge is not new to online advertising. However, high expectations for measurability are increasing the pressure to prove the contribution of online advertising to sales goals. Attribution models, which attempt to determine the contribution of individual touchpoints to a purchase, promise to provide a solution (Gaur & Barthi, 2020). However, the developments toward a post-cockie era outlined in Chap. 1 will further complicate or even prevent the necessary tracking.

We assume the following premises here:

- The described development toward a post-cockie era, in which third-party cockies are no longer used, will lead to an impoverishment of customer profiles.
- This makes it even more urgent for companies to build up their own database of customers.
- It will be even more difficult to prove the contribution of individual advertising measures to the purchase—especially for measures in the early phases of the customer journey.

Based on these considerations, the following consequences arise for the planning, implementation, and success monitoring of online campaigns:

1. Knowing your customers is increasingly becoming a key success factor in online advertising planning, and the development of meaningful buyer personas can help companies achieve this.
2. Companies need to develop sub-campaigns for each stage of the customer journey, each with its own set of campaign objectives that can be used to measure the success of advertising efforts.
3. In order to avoid getting lost in the details and to be able to allocate budgets to each stage of the customer journey, fundamental decisions need to be made up front.

This results in a three-stage structure for planning, implementing, and monitoring the success of online campaigns:

- Step 1: Fundamental decisions of the campaign.
- Step 2: Planning and implementing the sub-campaigns.
- Step 3: Success monitoring and optimization.

Following this basic structure, the following chapters describe the tasks involved in each case.

2.2 Step 1: Key Campaign Decisions

2.2.1 Clarifying the Starting Point and Objectives

When it comes to successful collaboration between a company and an advertising agency, the importance of a good briefing is often stressed. The briefing is a prerequisite for the agency to understand the company's initial situation and objectives. It contains the task and all the information that is considered necessary (Percy & Rosenbaum-Elliot, 2021). However, opinions differ on what information is necessary. "There are as many methods of briefing as there are people" (Davis, 2005, p. 173).

The information that should be included in a briefing can be divided into the following categories:

1. Initial Situation Information.

First of all, an agency needs information to understand the **company**, its **business model,** and its **position in the industry.**

Building on this, information is needed on the **market structure** and the **evolution of key market sizes.** It is therefore important to know the composition of the market (e.g., by segment, price category), whether and how strongly the market is growing and who the main competitors are (Percy & Rosenbaum-Elliot, 2021).

Information about the company's **previous communication and positioning** as well as the **positioning of its main competitors** is also helpful in order to gain a good understanding of the company's starting point.

2. Information About the Advertising Problem and Objectives.

The advertising problem is about understanding the **reason for a new campaign**: is there a new product to be launched, a new target group to be acquired, or is it stagnating sales? What are the objectives of the campaign? The question of objectives is particularly important. As we will see later, they need to be specified for each phase of the customer journey. At a higher level, this includes both economic advertising objectives (e.g., targeted sales figures or sales volumes) and psychological advertising objectives (e.g., desired positioning), as well as the central advertising message. The question of how this central message can be justified is also important (Percey & Rosenbaum-Elliot, 2021).

3. Target Group Information.

The **description of the target group** plays a central role in the briefing. Sociodemographic data (e.g., age, gender, income) as well as psychographic data (e.g., attitudes, interests) and behavioral characteristics (e.g., information, purchase and usage behavior) should be available. For online advertising in particular, a **buyer persona** and their **typical customer journey** should also be known. Due to the importance of this information for the online advertising planning, we will discuss it in more detail.

4. Budget and Schedule Information.

The size of the available **budget** has a significant impact on advertising options. It must take into account both the advertising objectives and the financial capabilities of the company. You also need to know how long you want to run the campaign and how you want to allocate the budget over that time.

Because of the importance of buyer personas and customer journeys in online campaign planning, both concepts are discussed in more detail below.

2.2.2 Developing the Buyer Personas

As described in Sect. 2.1.1, briefings always include information about the target audience. But why is this information often not enough for successful digital marketing and why do we recommend creating a buyer persona? To better understand, we will first look at the relationship between audiences and buyer personas and how to create meaningful buyer personas.

2.2.2.1 Connecting Target Groups and Buyer Personas

Differentiated and targeted marketing is an important prerequisite for successful marketing. For this reason, no marketing textbook can do without at least a brief explanation of the concept of market segmentation. Target groups are the result of market segmentation with the aim of uncovering differences in buyer behavior and gaining information for the use of marketing instruments. Closely related to target groups is the concept of buyer personas—also known as customer avatars—although the boundaries are often blurred. But what is the relationship between audiences and buyer personas, how do they differ, and why are buyer personas central to successful digital marketing?

Both concepts deal with the customers that a company wants to address with its services. While the concept of market segmentation was mentioned as early as 1956 (Smith, 1956), the concept of buyer personas is more recent. Its founder is Alan Cooper (1999), who as a software developer was faced with the challenge of designing the most user-friendly interfaces possible without knowing who would typically use the software. He solved the problem by conducting interviews with potential customers and summarizing the results in a persona (Vaclav, n.d.). Originally, the persona concept was not developed for marketing purposes, but as a tool for software and product design.

It is an archetypal representation of real or potential users. It's not a description of a real, individual, or average user. The persona represents patterns of user behavior, goals, and motivations, combined into a fictional description of a single individual. It also contains invented personal details to make the persona more "tangible and alive" for the development team (Blomkvist, 2002, p. 1).

The focus was on understanding the motives, goals, and behaviors of software users, which were enriched with additional personal details (e.g., name and age) to make the persona more tangible and alive for the development team.

In marketing, the value of such personas was quickly recognized—the benefit of a better understanding of customers' buying decisions, their motives, goals, and expectations for the communication and sales process. It is here, in the question of buying behavior, that the goals of both concepts meet; after all, market segmentation is also about uncovering differences in buyer behavior in order to gain information for the use of marketing instruments. There are several reasons why the information obtained in this way is often insufficient for further processing, especially in digital marketing:

- A key objective of market segmentation is to define the relevant total market for a product and to divide the (heterogeneous) total market into homogeneous submarkets. The criteria used to do this vary from industry to industry. However, the goal is always to find the criteria that best explain the differences in buying behavior (e.g., family life cycle, income situation, and risk appetite of the people a bank wants to attract as customers). The fact that it is not necessary to collect a "complete" customer profile is understandable from a cost-benefit perspective.
- An important part of market segmentation is the selection of the most attractive target group(s) for the company. Among other things, the market potential that can be reached with the target group must be estimated. This is one of the reasons why demographic (e.g., age, gender), geographic, and socioeconomic (e.g., occupation, income) criteria are used in market segmentation and target group description, in addition to the easier availability of this information.
- For traditional media planning, this target group information often already provides sufficient starting points, since the traditional (analog) media (TV, radio, magazines, etc.) publish user profiles with

information on demographic and socio-economic criteria that can be used as a basis for media selection.

However, in an increasingly "digitalized" market environment, this target information is not sufficient for the following reasons:

- As part of the customer journey, (potential) customers interact with the company through a variety of touchpoints (digital and physical). Information about which touchpoints are used in which phase of the customer journey and what expectations and problems customers have (gain and pain points) is not available from market segmentation.
- This lack of information hinders effective and efficient communication at each stage of the customer journey and hinders effective sales funnel management.
- In addition to the typical information about users of traditional media (demographic and socio-economic data), providers of digital channels (e.g., social media) offer a variety of other selection criteria for targeting. This information (e.g., about hobbies, relationship status, etc.) is missing from traditional audience descriptions.
- Before customers engage with a company, a large part of the customer journey may have been completed, i.e., a large part of the purchase decision may have been made. In this case, companies have already dropped out of the search grid of potential customers (or never appeared there in the first place) before they have had a chance to present the benefits of their own services. This makes it all the more important to know the triggers for when and why customers are considering a purchase for the first time.
- The more infrequently and infrequently companies and their employees come into contact with (potential) customers, the more important it is to have a clear picture of their buying motives, goals, expectations, and possible barriers to purchase in order to take them into account when creating content.

Market segmentation and the creation of buyer personas should not be seen as competing approaches. Rather, the target groups identified and selected through market segmentation are the starting point for the further development of buyer personas. Table 2.1 summarizes the main similarities and differences between the two approaches.

In the next chapter, we will show you how to create a buyer persona and what information you need to create one.

2.2.2.2 Create Buyer Personas

Fundamental Decision

The **starting point** for creating buyer personas is the **target group** selected by the company. For practical reasons, it is advisable to initially select only one target group to create a buyer persona. The following considerations should be taken into account:

1. Demographic (e.g., age, gender), socioeconomic (e.g., occupation, income), and motivational (e.g., retirement) criteria are often used to define market segments. Even when segments are easy to define and their size can be estimated, members of the target group may differ in their expectations and buying process. In this case, it may be useful and necessary for the company to create multiple buyer personas. Therefore, first check if there are multiple buyer personas within your selected audience, and then decide which buyer persona to create.
2. Buyer personas can be developed for different purposes, e.g., as a tool for developing new products and services or for planning communication and sales activities. It makes sense for the company to develop buyer personas that can be used for all these purposes; parallel development in R&D and marketing departments makes little sense and only leads to a waste of resources and confusion in the company. However, depending on which purpose is most important, you will analyze different aspects more closely (e.g., the touchpoints used in buyer personas for communication planning, or the product requirements and customer jobs in buyer personas for product development). So clarify which purpose is most important to you.

Table 2.1 Comparison of target audiences and buyer personas

	Target audiences	Buyer personas
Classification	Target groups are the result of market segmentation. It is used to identify differences in buyer behavior and to inform the use of marketing tools	Buyer personas are designed to help companies better understand their (potential) customers. They are mainly used in communication policy—selection of (digital) touchpoints, content marketing—and in product development
Background	The concept of market segmentation was first mentioned in the literature in 1956; a key objective is to divide the total market into homogeneous subsegments and select the most attractive target groups.	First mentioned in a book by Alan Cooper in 1999, personas were originally used as a tool for software development. Increasingly important in marketing, especially due to the specifics of digital marketing (customer journey, digital touchpoints, content marketing)
Definition	(Potential) buyers of a product who have similar demands on the product range and who react more homogeneously to the use of marketing instruments than the market as a whole	Model description of a fictitious person ("archetype") who represents a real target customer (desired customer) of the company
Criteria	A large number of criteria are available for market segmentation and target group identification. The criteria that best explain the differences in buying behavior are selected	Bundles of criteria are used to create a buyer persona. There is no one set of guidelines for which criteria to use. Typical criteria include goals and motivations, needs and usage profile, benefits and pain points, barriers and roles in the buying process, touchpoints, and "classic" demographic and socioeconomic criteria from market segmentation

Example The group of DINKS (Double Income No Kids), i.e., childless couples living in a joint household where both partners are employed, will comprise about 8.72 million people in Germany in 2022. The DINKS group has an above-average household net income: while on average 42.3% of the population in Germany has a household net income of more than €3500, the figure for DINKS is 62.6%. Almost 80% of DINKS in Germany have a household net income of more than €3000. The largest age group is 50 to 59 years old, with about 1/3 of DINKS in this age group. Another 20% are in the 30–39 age group (Statista, 2022a, b).

If a bank wants to segment the market in order to identify an interesting target group for investment products, the segmentation criteria "age," "family life cycle," " household net income" and "motive" could be defined as follows: DINKS between the ages of 30 and 39 with a household net income above €3500 and the motive of "retirement planning."

However, a closer look reveals that this target group, defined according to demographic, socio-economic, and motivational criteria, is not very homogeneous in terms of its expectations of investment products and the advisory services provided by a bank. For example, clients' expectations may be influenced by their personal risk tolerance (low to high) and their level of knowledge about financial products (low to high). Combining these criteria results in a matrix with four quadrants. People in the "low risk tolerance" and "little experience with financial products" quadrants are likely to differ from people in the "high risk tolerance" and "extensive experience with financial products" quadrants.

When creating buyer personas, it makes sense to create a buyer persona for each of these four quadrants. In practice, it makes sense to start with the quadrant that is most important to the company.

Another important decision is whether the buyer persona will be used primarily for developing product and consulting offerings or primarily for planning communication activities.

Criteria for Creating Buyer Personas

In the literature, there is no uniform description of the criteria necessary for the creation of buyer personas. As a result, there is a wide variety of templates available. It is important to keep in mind that buyer personas are supposed to represent the ideal customer of a company, and that expectations and buying processes differ from industry to industry and from target group to target group. Standardized templates therefore run the risk of missing important details. For this reason, the starting point for creating buyer personas should be the question, "What should the criteria be used for?"

1. Why Does the Customer Engage with the Product/Service?

This question addresses two aspects: (a) What is the **trigger** for the customer to become interested in the product/service right now? External triggers can often be observed, such as

- Changes in personal circumstances (e.g., relocation, marriage or separation, birth of a child, a birthday).
- Changes in socio-economic circumstances (e.g., completion of education, career change, promotion, change in income, payment of life insurance).
- Expiration of a contract (e.g., cell phone, insurance).
- Dissatisfaction with an existing product/service.
- Recommendations from third parties (e.g., family, friends, colleagues, and acquaintances).

So ask yourself what, in your industry, is a specific trigger for customers to consider buying a product. These can be trivial triggers (such as hunger when buying a ready-made pizza in the case of impulse purchases). On the other hand, in the case of purchase decisions that also involve a (lengthy) search for information and product comparisons, a variety of triggers are conceivable. For example, the birth of a child, a salary increase, or the expiration of a leasing contract could all be reasons to look for a new car. The better you know your customer's trigger(s), the better you can tailor your communication efforts.

The second aspect to consider is (b) **customer motivation**. A good starting point for understanding customer buying motivations is the customer job or "job to be done" (Christensen et al., 2016). The "job" or "customer job" stands for the result or goal that the customer wants to achieve with the product or service. This is not just about the

- functional job (the actual problem that is to be solved), but also about the,
- emotional job, which is related to how someone wants to feel about owning or using the product, and the,
- social job, which is related to how someone wants to be seen by others by owning or using the product (Osterwalder et al., 2014).

A product or service can certainly fulfill all three types of jobs for customers, e.g., when buying an electric car, not only the functional job plays a role, but also the emotional job (e.g., the good feeling of no longer needing fossil fuels) and the social job (e.g., the image of being an environmentally conscious person). Emotional jobs are also important in B2B marketing, e.g., choosing the market leader's software solution can provide a sense of security ("there will be no problems with this"). Social jobs (e.g., being perceived as a sustainable company by customers and employees) may also play an increasingly important role in purchasing decisions.

2. What Do Customers Expect from the Product/Service?

Closely related to the motives or (customer) jobs are the **expectations** and **requirements** that the buyer persona places on the product/service. According to the Kano model of customer satisfaction (Vitale et al., 2010), the requirements of the buyer persona can be divided into basic requirements, performance requirements, and enthusiasm requirements.

- Customers' basic requirements refer to features of your product or service that are taken for granted. If they are met, customers are not satisfied; if they are not met, they are dissatisfied.
- Customers' performance needs can lead to both satisfaction and dissatisfaction, depending on how well they are met.
- Enthusiasm requirements, on the other hand, do not lead to dissatisfaction if they are not met. However, when they are met, they lead to very high customer satisfaction or enthusiasm.

A comparison with the industry standard also helps to identify what can be considered basic and performance features. Interviews with customers are a good way to identify possible excitement features and to uncover previously unresolved problems or problems that customers have not yet articulated ("latent").

To gain a good understanding of customer needs, it may also be useful to examine the buyer persona's usage profile and experience with the product or product category. For example, in the case of electric cars, it makes a difference whether someone uses the car mainly for short trips and in city traffic, or whether they regularly drive longer distances. In the latter case, the issue of "range anxiety" will play a greater role, and again it makes a difference whether someone has experience with electric cars or is considering buying one for the first time.

3. What Can Prevent Customers from Buying the Product/Service?

While "gain points" (benefit expectations) are considered when clarifying customer needs, the question of barriers to purchase is about "pain points." Pain points can also help to better understand customer expectations. Here, however, they should help identify the reasons why the buyer persona has not yet purchased the product/service (i.e., what has prevented them from doing so) or what might prevent the buyer persona from making a purchase decision now.

The logic of functional, emotional, and social customer jobs can also help here: Concerns about the functional task ("Does it really work this way?," "Does it really solve my problem?"), an emotional dilemma ("Should I really spend so much money on this product?"), or the fear of negative reactions from the social environment ("What will XY say about this?") may represent problems and risks that prevent the buyer persona from buying. To identify possible barriers, it may be helpful to consider the buyer persona's environment or the environment in which the product will be used.

Example Barriers that prevent a buyer persona from making a purchase may also be environmental (e.g., housing).

- A potential buyer will not even consider an electric car because he lives in an apartment and does not see a way to charge the car at home. In order to interest this potential buyer in his own product, a supplier would also have to show solutions for how this person could charge the vehicle at home.
- A person who would like to bake at home for a special occasion decides not to because she doesn't have the baking utensils. A supplier of baking ingredients would need to provide solutions in its recipes to replace the missing baking utensils.

4. **Who Influences the Buyer Persona's Purchase Decision?**

Even in business-to-consumer marketing, it should not be assumed without verification that the purchase of a product or service is always an individual decision of the buyer persona.

- Even in the private sphere, people are influenced by friends and acquaintances. The aforementioned social benefits of a product suggest that it may be important to the buyer persona how they are perceived by others as a result of owning the product or brand. Products for which peer influence is particularly important are those that are visibly consumed/used—from clothing and sports equipment to mobile devices (smartphone, laptop, tablet) and vehicles.
- The buyer persona may also actively seek advice or suggestions from others when uncertain about the purchase decision. This subjective uncertainty may be due to a variety of reasons (e.g., lack of experience

with the product). Opinion leaders in the person's environment and influencers in social media play an important role.
- When major purchases are made by families (e.g., buying a new car, furniture, or vacations), it is possible that the buyer persona's purchase decision is strongly influenced by other family members or even made together as a family.

In business-to-business marketing, the purchase decision is usually not made by one person (e.g., the buyer) alone. Depending on the degree of novelty of a purchase, the associated organizational consequences, or simply the amount of the purchase price, different people are involved in the purchase decision. They can be grouped in a buying center, which may consist of the following roles (Vitale et al., 2010):

- The buyer is the person in the company who receives the offers and is responsible for the economic processing of the purchase; he is often located in the purchasing department and is comparatively easy to identify.
- The user is the person in the organization who will work with the purchased service (e.g., product, software, etc.); he or she is also usually easy to identify.
- The decider is the person in the organization who makes the purchase decision based on his or her position in the organization's hierarchy; depending on the size of the organization and the amount of the acquisition cost, this may be a department head, an authorized signatory, or the CEO.
- Influencers are people who have an influence on the final decision of the decision maker; influencers are more difficult to identify as they can come from within the company as well as from the company's environment (e.g., consultants, business friends).
- Gatekeepers (information selectors) are people who control access to the decision-maker to some extent and can control the flow of information in the buying center; for example, management assistants can be considered gatekeepers.

5. What Channels Can I Use to Reach the Persona?

To engage the persona in the buying process, you need to know the channels they use: What social media are they on, do they use traditional media such as newspapers, magazines, radio, or TV? In short, which traditional and digital touchpoints can be used to reach the buyer persona?

Of course, the so-called digital "paid touchpoints" are relevant to the topic of this book, i.e., the channels through which the buyer persona can be reached with advertising measures (e.g., social media advertising, search engine advertising, or digital display advertising).

The Minimum Viable Persona (MVP) as a Starting Point

Creating a buyer persona requires a great deal of information. Much of this information is gathered through qualitative interviews with potential and actual buyers or customer-facing employees. This can be a long, time-consuming process. At the same time, however, advertising campaigns in digital channels offer the opportunity to learn more about the buyer persona on an ongoing basis.

With this in mind, the question arises as to what information is needed to start planning online advertising. To answer this question, it makes sense to borrow from the concept of the "minimum viable product": a minimum viable product is a product/service that is at such an early stage of development that it contains only the functionality needed for the actual purpose. It "… is comprised of the least amount of functionality necessary to solve a problem sufficiently such that your customer will engage with your product and even pay you for it, if that's your revenue model" (Cooper & Vlaskovits, 2013). The minimum viable persona can be enriched with insights from the advertising campaigns carried out in order to gradually gain a more detailed picture of the buyer persona.

Definition As with the minimum viable product, the minimum viable persona contains only the information necessary for the initial planning of a digital advertising campaign.

So what is the purpose of buyer personas in online advertising? We see three roles they should play:

- Gain insight into the design of the advertising message at each stage of the customer journey.
- Selecting appropriate touchpoints for each stage of the customer journey.
- Obtaining information for the placement of advertising in the digital channels, i.e., for the selection of the target group in the digital channels (targeting).

What information is needed to create a minimum viable persona? We recommend collecting the following information about the buyer persona:

1. **Demographic Data About the Persona.**
    When selecting the audience to which online advertising is to be delivered, each digital platform and channel offers different options for selecting the demographics of people, such as

- Gender.
- Age.
- The region in which the ad is to be displayed.
- Job-related criteria (such as work experience, education).

    This information is always required to set up the basic settings for selecting the target group to be reached by the ad campaign. In addition, depending on the platform, there may be a number of other selection options, such as relationship status or the company a person works for (e.g., in terms of industry and company size). Before selecting such criteria, one should critically question whether reliable information is actually available, whether plausibility considerations are being followed, or whether speculation is involved.

2. **Persona Interests.**

    A unique feature of digital channels is the ability to target audiences based on their interests. For this reason, an MVP should include information about the interests of the target audience.

3. **Customer Journey and Preferred Digital Channels (Touchpoints) of the Persona.**

    The customer journey maps the customer's information search and purchase process—from the first impulse or initial interest in buying a product/service, through the pre-purchase and purchase phases, to the post-purchase phase.

    The customer journey is influenced by characteristics of the persona itself (e.g., their experience with the product) as well as the product category (e.g., high or low price). Related to the customer journey is the question of the persona's preferred digital channels. This information is needed to select the touchpoints through which the persona should be engaged at each stage of the customer journey.

4. **Pain Points and Needs of the Persona.**

    In order to formulate specific messages that are relevant to the buyer persona at each stage of the customer journey, information about the expectations and possible pain points of potential customers is required.

The points mentioned so far—demographics, interests, customer journey, and touchpoints—are needed to select the right channels and make the most important settings for targeting. With information about the specific pain points and expectations of the persona at each stage of the customer journey, it is possible to formulate specific messages that are relevant to the buyer persona.

The criteria mentioned here need to be further specified depending on the platform on which the online advertising is to be displayed. The level of detail required will vary depending on the data collected about the user and the targeting options offered.

2.2.3 Definition of Customer Journey and Campaign Groups

2.2.3.1 Basic Considerations

The development of the customer journey is closely linked to the creation of the buyer persona. While the buyer persona represents a "snapshot" of the typical customer, the customer journey looks at the information search and purchase process of that persona. Knowledge of the customer journey is relevant to online advertising planning for two reasons:

- On the one hand, it makes it possible to select the relevant touchpoints for the different stages of the buying process based on the media that the buyer persona generally uses.
- On the other hand, it helps to shape the content of the advertising message; depending on where the customer is in the buying process, different messages will be required to ensure that your company is given further consideration and that a purchase is ultimately made.

When planning your online advertising, we recommend proceeding in a two-step approach:

1. Define the customer journey.
2. Define campaign groups.

2.2.3.2 Defining the Customer Journey

The customer journey is a metaphor for the customer's information-seeking and buying process and therefore needs to be adapted to the specific industry and type of buying decision. We recommend the following steps to create the customer journey:

1. Define the buyer persona.
2. Clarify the stages of the customer journey.
3. Describe the steps of the buyer persona in the phases.

4. Clarify the gain and pain points in each phase.
5. Identify the key touchpoints in each stage.

In Sect. 2.1.2, we explained how to create the buyer persona and what information you need. Therefore, we will cover steps 2 through 5 here. It should be noted that the steps cannot always be followed in a strictly linear fashion. In particular, steps 3, 4, and 5 are closely related, as they are collected, for example, during customer interviews.

Phases of the Customer Journey

In principle, the customer journey consists of pre-purchase, purchase, and post-purchase phases. In the literature and in practice, there are many different approaches to further subdivide these phases. The main difference is in how the pre-purchase phase is defined. The central question here is: How intensely do customers engage in the purchase decision?

To answer this question, it is helpful to look at customer involvement in a purchase decision. Involvement refers to the degree of subjectively perceived importance of a behavior (Akhoondnejad et al., 2024). When customers are intensely involved in a purchase, it is referred to as high involvement, otherwise it is referred to as low involvement (Lischka & Prohst, 2018). Depending on the level of involvement, the pre-purchase phase therefore varies in length (cf. Table 2.2).

It is important to keep in mind that involvement is not only dependent on the product, but also on situational factors (e.g., the urgency of a purchase) or personality traits. In principle, customers with low involvement can hardly be convinced by arguments, while high involvement requires very good arguments (Michaelidou & Dibb, 2008).

Based on Kotler et al. (2017), the basic phases of the customer journey can be defined as in Fig. 2.1.

Steps of the Buyer Persona in the Stages

Next, describe what the buyer persona does at each stage. What information does he look for, what channels does he use, and who does he talk to? The answers to these questions will be influenced by factors such as

Table 2.2 Involvement and customer journey

	Typical low-involvement products	Typical high-involvement products
Features	Lower price Lower risk of making the wrong decision Less variation in quality between vendor offerings Less need for explanation	Higher price Higher risk of making the wrong decision Large differences in quality between vendor offerings Greater need for explanation
Examples	Mineral water, potato chips, office supplies, household cleaners, etc.	Computers, cars, bicycles, further education, insurance, etc.
Behavior of the customer	Customers are rarely actively involved in the purchase decision Customers need little information Frequent impulse or repeat purchases	Customers are actively involved in the purchase decision Customers need more information
Consequence for the pre-purchase phase of the customer journey	In the pre-purchase phase, the main focus is on building brand awareness of the brand and sympathy for the brand	The pre-purchase phase takes longer and involves a more detailed evaluation of the alternatives

- The buyer persona's involvement.
- How well they know their company.
- How well they know the product/service itself.
- The touchpoints the buyer persona typically uses.
- Where the persona is in the customer journey.

Keep in mind that the information you need may be related not only to the product or service, but also to your company itself, or to relevant conditions (e.g., delivery times).

Gain and Pain Points in the Stages

In Sect. 2.1.2, we discussed the importance of gains and pains when creating the buyer persona. What does the persona expect (gains) and what

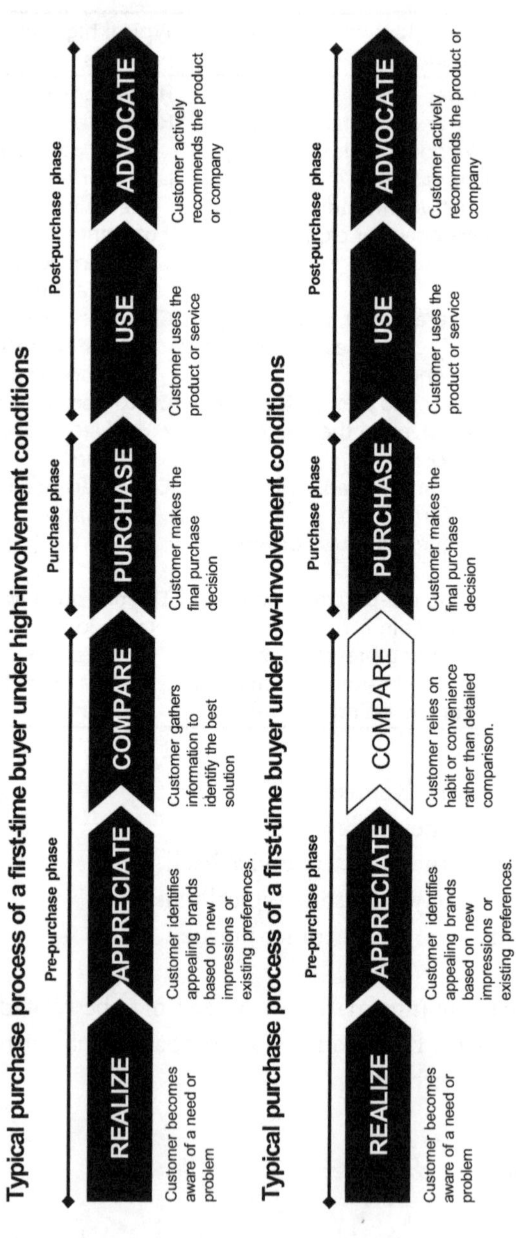

Typical purchase process of a first-time buyer under high-involvement conditions

Pre-purchase phase			Purchase phase	Post-purchase phase	
REALIZE	APPRECIATE	COMPARE	PURCHASE	USE	ADVOCATE
Customer becomes aware of a need or problem	Customer identifies appealing brands based on new impressions or existing preferences.	Customer gathers information to identify the best solution	Customer makes the final purchase decision	Customer uses the product or service	Customer actively recommends the product or company

Typical purchase process of a first-time buyer under low-involvement conditions

Pre-purchase phase			Purchase phase	Post-purchase phase	
REALIZE	APPRECIATE	COMPARE	PURCHASE	USE	ADVOCATE
Customer becomes aware of a need or problem	Customer identifies appealing brands based on new impressions or existing preferences.	Customer relies on habit or convenience rather than detailed comparison.	Customer makes the final purchase decision	Customer uses the product or service	Customer actively recommends the product or company

Fig. 2.1 Phases of the customer journey considering customer involvement

might prevent them from buying (pains)? The next step is to map these gains and pains to each stage of the buying process. This helps to identify ideas for specific communication messages.

Example Manufacturers of electric cars know that range is an important criterion for customers when deciding for or against a supplier (gain point). And due to "range anxiety," it can also be a reason why potential customers decide against an electric car (pain point). This also explains why the range of the vehicle plays an important role in the appeal and ask phase of the application.

What is not considered, however, is a pain point that may prevent a certain target group from even seriously considering buying an EV: People who live in apartments and have no way of installing their own charging station. In order for this target group to even "start" the customer journey for an EV, a provider would have to address this problem in the awareness phase and promise a solution.

An important goal when planning communications is to ensure that prospects consider your company in the next phase of the customer journey or do not abandon the customer journey. To do this, it is necessary to communicate "phase-specific" benefits and pain points.

Key Touchpoints Throughout the Stages

When you created the buyer persona, you already identified the media they prefer to use. The next step is to map these media to each stage. When planning online advertising, the focus is on paid touchpoints. This includes all forms of advertising whose distribution incurs costs, e.g., search engine advertising, online and social media advertising (Baxendale et al., 2015).

2.2.3.3 Defining Campaign Groups

The next step is to define different campaign groups for planning online advertising. The following basic considerations apply:

1. It is difficult to reach different buyer personas with one campaign. A single campaign would effectively lump all personas into one group, making it difficult to tailor content and messaging to the needs and pain points of each persona.
2. At each stage of the customer journey, different sub-goals need to be achieved to keep the buyer persona considering your company in the next stage of the customer journey.

> **Important**
> Define a **campaign group** for each buyer persona. Each campaign group consists of **sub-campaigns** for the each pre-buy stage (Aware, Appeal, Ask) of the customer journey. For each of these sub-campaigns, define separate **objectives** to be achieved by the advertising, as well as key performance indicators (**KPIs**) that can be used to measure success.

This basic consideration is illustrated in the following example.

Example An e-bike manufacturer has identified two target groups for its new e-mountain bike, each represented by two personas.

- **First-time buyers** who currently ride a conventional mountain bike and have no information about what makes a good e-bike and what to look for when buying one.
- **E-bike riders who currently ride a competitor's product**. This target group is thinking about buying a new e-bike and currently only knows the manufacturer of their own e-bike. They already have extensive product experience and know what to look for when making a purchase.

Looking at the customer journeys of the two personas, it is clear that the manufacturer needs to achieve different goals in its campaigns in order to be considered in the further purchase process. Accordingly, different messages need to be delivered and different online channels used.

Persona 1
The awareness phase is not just about making your brand known. First, the persona needs to be made aware of the benefits of an e-bike and get interested in this product group.

As the persona is not yet familiar with the brand and is probably not actively looking for e-bikes, advertising on the Google Display Network, YouTube, and Facebook would be suitable for generating interest. A possible message here would be the benefits of an e-bike (e.g., more rides because the uphill rides are less strenuous).

The Appeal phase is about building the image of your own brand; the platforms Instagram and YouTube are suitable for this, for example, with emotionally powerful (short) videos.

In the subsequent **Ask phase**, the persona searches more specifically for important product features of e-bikes, in this case Google Ads and again YouTube ads can be placed.

Persona 2

In contrast to Persona 1, the goal in the **Awareness phase** is simply to increase brand awareness. Since the persona is already actively searching for information, search engine advertising (e.g., Google Ads) would be an appropriate measure.

As with persona 1, the **Appeal phase** is about building your own brand image. Emotional (short) videos on Instagram and YouTube can also be used here. Depending on the motivations of the personas, the videos can be somewhat different.

In the **Ask phase**, Persona 2 also conducts more targeted research, although their search queries will differ from those of Persona 1 due to their greater product knowledge. This, in turn, must be taken into account in the keywords used in search engine advertising.

The following figure summarizes the example graphically (see Fig. 2.2).

2.2.4 Budgeting

The definition of campaign groups raises two issues. One is how to distribute the total budget among the various sub-campaigns, and the other is how to determine the amount of budget available. In principle, there are several ways to determine the budget; the most commonly used approaches in practice are the

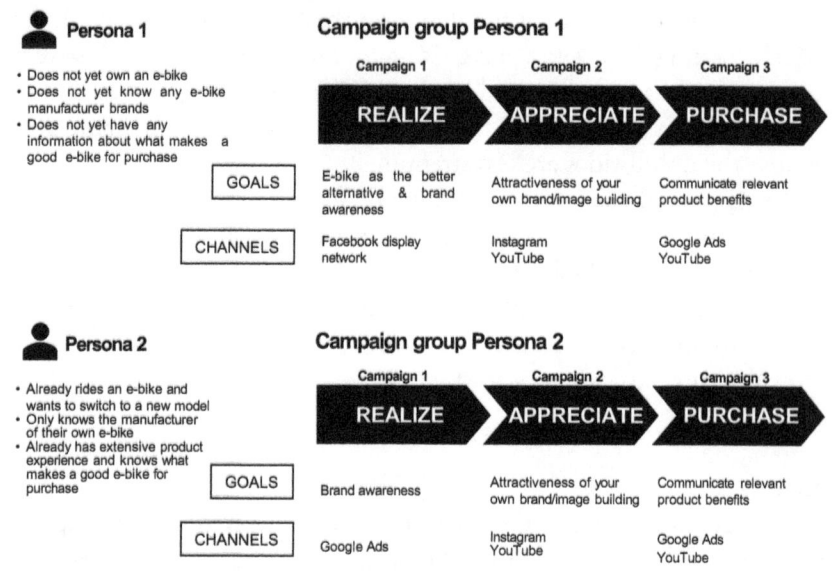

Fig. 2.2 Campaign groups and sub-campaigns

- Percentage of sales method.
- Communication costs per unit of sales method.
- Update method (i.e., based on previous periods).
- Financial sustainability method.
- Competitive parity method ("share-of-advertising," "share-of-voice").
- Market share method (Kolsarici et al., 2020).

The advantage of these approaches is their practicality and ease of application. However, this should not obscure a number of weaknesses that they entail, which is why an orientation toward the tasks and goals of communication is recommended.

The amounts invested in advertising in the past (extrapolation method) in conjunction with the forecast sales (percentage of sales method or communication costs per sales unit method) and the financial sustainability method can provide an orientation framework in the sense of an upper limit. In addition, the budget required for all campaign groups can be roughly estimated. It results from the following parameters:

1. The reach of the campaign, i.e., the number of people to be reached by the campaign,
2. Advertising pressure, i.e., the required contact frequency during the campaign period.
3. Media cost, i.e., the cost of advertising placements in online media.

When planning an online campaign, there is a trade-off between reach and exposure during the campaign period. If the advertising budget remains the same, a higher target reach leads to a lower contact frequency with the advertising material; conversely, a higher contact frequency automatically means that the reach must be limited.

For this reason, it is particularly important to estimate how many times a target person needs to be exposed to the advertising message in order to learn it and achieve the advertising goal. The required advertising pressure is influenced by the following factors, among others:

- Advertising pressure from competitors.
- Complexity of the message.
- Interest of the target group in the content of the advertising message.
- Use of synergy effects in your own communication.
- Extent of the desired behavioral change (Fuchs & Unger, 2014; Kolsarici et al., 2020).

The multitude of these factors shows that there is no universal "right" number of contacts that can be applied to all campaigns and contexts. It is also important to distinguish between actual ad media contacts and OTS (opportunities to see) (Czinkota et al., 2021). Not every opportunity to see leads to an actual contact.

Media costs depend on the medium chosen and are traditionally expressed as cost per thousand (CPM) or cost per mille (CPM). The CPM indicates the price to be paid to reach 1000 people with a medium (Kreutzer, 2023). It is calculated using the formula "price of the ad divided by reach times 1000". This makes it possible to compare the cost of advertising through different media.

CPM also plays an important role in online advertising, although there are different billing models available for online media. Depending on the goal of an online campaign, there are different billing models available to effectively plan and optimize online advertising strategies across the entire customer journey:

1. **Awareness Phase.**

   - Cost Per Mille (CPM): This model calculates the cost per thousand ad impressions. It is suitable for advertising campaigns that aim to increase the visibility and awareness of a brand or product.
   - Cost Per Engagement (CPE): With the CPE model, advertisers pay for specific user interactions with the ad, such as filling out a form or watching a video.

2. **Appeal Phase.**

   - Cost Per View (CPV): In this model, advertisers pay for the number of video views or interactions with their video ad. It is ideal for brands that want to create an emotional connection with users through video content.
   - Cost Per Engagement (CPE): With the CPE model, advertisers pay for specific user interactions with the ad, such as filling out a form or watching a video.

3. **Ask** Phase.

   - Cost Per Click (CPC): With the CPC model, advertisers pay for each click their ad receives. It is particularly suitable for campaigns that are designed to drive traffic to a website and encourage users to learn more about the company's offerings.
   - Cost Per Lead (CPL): This payment model (also known as pay per lead) is used in affiliate marketing. The advertiser pays when a specific action (such as describing to a newsletter) has been triggered.

4. **Purchase Phase:**

   - Cost Per Acquisition (CPA): The CPA model is performance-based and advertisers pay for each specific action, such as a sale or a registration. It works well for campaigns that have clear conversion goals.

Detailed information on the available billing models and costs can be found in the online platform media kits.

Example The video platform YouTube reaches 49 million adults per month in Germany. The media kit for the second half of 2022 includes the following CPMs for various video solutions (Table 2.3).

Another key decision is how to allocate the budget over the duration of the campaign. The first question is whether the campaign should be

Table 2.3 CPM of selected video solutions on YouTube (Germany, second half of 2022; Source: Google, August 2022)

Marketing objective	Video solution	Purchasing workflow	Bids and prices
Reach and brand awareness	Video Masthead Space on the YouTube home page and in the home feed	Fixed CPM	€ 5.20 CPM Run of Network + € 0.80 Targeting surcharge
	Bumper Ads Non-skippable 6-sec video	Auction-based & Instant Reserve	€ 3.00 to € 5.50 CPM
	TrueView for Reach Skippable video display, unlimited length	Auction-based only	€ 0.01 to € 0.04 CPV (cost per view)
Consideration—building willingness to buy	TrueView In-Stream Skippable video ad; payment is only required when users watch or interact with the ad	Auction-based only	€ 0.01 to € 0.04 CPV (cost per view)
	In-Feed Video for Consideration Click-to-play video display	Auction-based only	€ 0.04 to € 0.09 CPV (cost per view)
Action	Video Action Campaign Skippable video ads that promote lower-funnel actions (e.g., website clicks)	Auction-based only	CPM varies; target CPA (cost per action), max conversions

concentrated in a shorter period of time or spread out over a longer period of time. If the budget is to be distributed over a longer period of time, the following options are available:

- Constant distribution is ideal for reminder advertising, e.g., if the brand is already known to the target group.
- With increasing intensity, the advertising pressure increases over time, which makes sense if the focus is on a specific event (e.g., a seasonal event or a product launch).
- With decreasing intensity, the advertising pressure decreases over time, which can be useful, for example, in a follow-up campaign for a new product launch (Esch & Winter, 2009; Kotler et al. 2021).

2.3 Step 2: Plan and Execute the Sub-campaigns at Each Stage of the Customer Journey

For each stage of the customer journey, a sub-campaign is planned and executed based on a specific persona. The tasks involved are described in this chapter.

2.3.1 Planning Basis for the Sub-campaigns

The following information from Step 1—Basic Decisions for Campaign Planning—is available for planning the sub-campaigns in the individual phases of the customer journey:

- Basic information about the buyer persona—the minimum viable persona (Sect. 2.2.2.2.3), which includes the touchpoints that can be used to reach the persona.
- The objectives to be achieved with the campaign groups at each stage of the customer journey (Sect. 2.2.3.3).
- The budget available for each campaign group (Sect. 2.2.4).

On this basis, the following tasks for planning and implementing the sub-campaigns can now be undertaken:

1. Media planning, i.e., selecting the channels on which the online advertising will be displayed.
2. Design of the advertising material.
3. Placement of advertising.

2.3.2 Media Planning—Channel Selection

For each sub-campaign, the first step is to determine the channels through which the target audience will be reached. The basis for this is provided by the minimum viable persona developed (Sect. 2.2.2.2.3). Based on this, the following questions need to be answered:

- Is the ad primarily mobile or desktop?
- Which online environment will be used to display the ad?
- What ad formats should be used?

2.3.2.1 Mobile or Desktop Advertising

Based on the information about the buyer persona, it is known whether the target group is better reached via mobile or desktop advertising. It can be seen here that mobile advertising will be ahead of desktop advertising from 2019: the share of mobile advertising in global advertising revenue will be around 61% in 2022 (Statista, 2022b).

Ad creative requirements may differ depending on whether the ad is to be served on mobile or desktop. The main differences are as follows:

1. **Ad Size and Format.**
   Due to different screen sizes and resolutions, ads need to be designed differently for desktop and mobile devices. Desktop ads can be larger and more detailed, while mobile ads need to be optimized for smaller

screens. For mobile devices, the "medium rectangle" (300 × 250 pixels) is a common format chosen because it provides a large enough area to display visuals and messages clearly and attractively.
2. **Ad Positioning.**
   On desktops, ads can also be displayed in side columns, headers, or as an overlay. Mobile ads, on the other hand, are often embedded or scrollable due to limited screen real estate.
3. **User Interaction.**
   The way users interact with ads can also differ. Mobile devices tend to be touch-based, while desktop devices use a mouse. This can affect the design of call-to-action elements.
4. **In-app vs. Web Advertising.**
   Desktop ads typically appear in the browser while users are browsing the web. However, in addition to the mobile web, there is another option for mobile advertising: in-app advertising. These are ads that are placed within mobile applications (apps). They can come in a variety of formats, such as banners, interstitials, or video ads. In-app advertising can also include interactive elements to encourage users to interact and can take into account other information about the user (e.g., preferences or location data).

Depending on the format chosen, there are additional requirements for the design of the ad creative.

2.3.2.2 Choice of Online Environment

For the distribution of online advertising, companies have different online environments (advertising channels) at their disposal, which can be structured as in Table 2.4.

Depending on the type of online environment you want to advertise in, there are different ad formats available.

2.3.2.3 Choice of Ad Formats

The available advertising formats refer to the various forms of **display advertising** (also known as display advertising, banner advertising or

Table 2.4 Online environments (advertising channels) for digital advertising

Search engine networks	Google Display Network
	Microsoft Audience Network (Bing Ads)
Publisher websites of publishing houses	Spiegel Online, Zeit-Online
Blogs	TechCrunch, Mashable, t3n
Social networks	Facebook, Instagram, LinkedIn, Tiktok, Xing, YouTube
Programmatic advertising platforms	Real-time bidding platforms such as DoubleClick or AppNexus
Retargeting platforms	AdRoll, Criteo
Comparison and rating portals	Check24, Trustpilot
Content aggregators	Reddit, BuzzFeed
Online retailer	Amazon
Mobile apps	In-app advertising in games (e.g., Candy Crush) or news apps such as n-tv

Source: Author

display marketing). Display advertising refers to the "[...] placement of graphic advertising media on websites or applications on mobile devices for commercial purposes" (Arholdt et al., 2023, p. 11; Jolaoso, 2023).

Originally understood as banner advertising on websites, it is now also used in social media (social display advertising) or on Amazon. Video formats are a growth driver for display advertising. OVK estimates that display advertising revenues in Germany will reach € 5.467 billion in 2023, with video formats accounting for almost 40% (i.e., +14 percentage points compared to 2022) (BVWD, 2023).

The most common advertising formats in display advertising are listed below:

- **Banners**, which convey the advertising message with text and images and are available in different sizes. Banners can be both static and interactive (HTML5 banners). They can include video, audio, interactivity, and other multimedia content.
- **Content ads** are specialized ad formats that are embedded within the editorial content of a website, often in the form of nearly square banners surrounded by text. Their design and message are often designed to blend in with the surrounding content. As a result, they are perceived as less intrusive by the user and are often not recognizable as an

ad at first glance. Content ads are therefore classified as native advertising, which includes any type of advertising that is designed to blend seamlessly into the environment in which it is placed. This can be editorial content, social media, or other platforms.

- **In-stream advertising**, where video advertising is placed within a video stream, typically before (pre-roll), during (mid-roll), or after (post-roll) the main video. Platforms that use in-stream advertising include YouTube and Vimeo.
- **Out-stream ads** (standalone video ads) placed outside of a video stream. These ads can appear on web pages between paragraphs of text, in a page element, on social media, or in other places where there is no main video. This type of ad often starts autoplaying (with or without sound) when it is visible on the screen and pauses when it is not. They provide an additional way to monetize video content and extend the reach of video advertising beyond traditional video platforms.

Each of these formats mentioned has specific advantages and disadvantages (Table 2.5), which must be weighed by the advertiser.

2.3.3 Design of Advertising Material

2.3.3.1 Design Principles

Various design elements are available for the content and graphic design of the advertising formats (text, image, moving image, audio), which can be combined with each other. Their use depends on the type of banner (static, interactive, rich media, video) and the size of the banner used.

Banner Sizes

The first decision when designing an advertising banner is the choice of banner size. Each publisher and each platform on which you can advertise has its own guidelines. Google, for example, specifies no less than 52 different banner sizes for display ads and 66 banner sizes for app ads in its

Table 2.5 Pros and cons of ad formats

Advertising format	Advantages	Disadvantages
Static advertising banners	Easy and quick to create; Cost effective; Clear and direct message; Good readability; Fast load times	Low engagement (click rate); Limited information; Also easier to overlook
Interactive advertising banners	Higher engagement through interactivity; ability to integrate different media; rich in information	More complex and time-consuming to create; potentially higher cost; longer load times
Animated advertising banners	Interactivity; high attention through multimedia elements; possibility of advanced animations	Complex to create; Higher cost; May have longer load times; Possible compatibility issues with browsers
Content ads	Contextual; better integration with content; higher user acceptance	May be less prominent, depending on the quality and relevance of the content
In-stream advertising	High visibility; users are more attentive; good placement in videos; opportunity for targeted advertising	May be perceived as annoying; interruption of video content; possible use of ad blockers
Out-stream advertising	More flexible placement; does not interfere with video content; ability to reach users outside of video platforms	May receive less attention than in-stream, depending on placement and surrounding content
Static advertising banners	Easy and quick to create; Cost effective; Clear and direct message; Good readability; Fast load times	Low engagement (click rate); Limited information; Also easier to overlook

Google Ads Editor (Google Ads Editor Help). The variety of banner formats can basically be structured as in Table 2.6.

With Google Responsive Search Ads, advertisers can create multiple headlines and descriptions, which Google then combines and tests to determine the most effective versions. With up to 15 headlines and 4 descriptions, the system automatically prioritizes the highest-performing combinations, improving relevance by matching ads to users' search queries. Benefits include increased click-through rates (CTR), time and cost savings through automated optimization, and increased reach as ads adapt to different search terms (Sharma, 2023).

Table 2.6 Common banner formats

Banner format	Features	Advantages	Disadvantages
Square ads	Square banners with the same width and height Popular sizes are 250 × 250 or 200 × 200 pixels	Flexible placement on the site and in social media Symmetrical dimensions are aesthetically pleasing	Limited space for advertising content and creative design compared to wider formats
Rectangle	Rectangular banners that are wider than they are high Popular sizes are 300 × 250 or 336 × 280 pixels	Offers more space for text and graphics than square banners.	Can interrupt the reading flow on a web page if it is not well placed
Skyscraper	Narrow, high banners that are often positioned at the edge of the page Popular sizes are 120 × 600 (standard skyscraper) and 160 × 600 pixels (wide skyscraper)	Takes up little horizontal space, good for side rails	May not display as well on mobile devices Less conspicuous than wider formats
Leaderboard	Wide, flat banners that are often placed at the top of a website Popular sizes are 728 × 90 pixels (super banner) or 468 × 60 (full banner)	Clearly visible when placed at the top of the page Offers plenty of space for text and graphics	May not display as well on mobile devices
Mobile	Banners for use on mobile devices Popular size is 320 × 480 pixels	Optimized for use on mobile devices	Limited space for advertising content and creative design

(*continued*)

Table 2.6 (continued)

Banner format	Features	Advantages	Disadvantages
Large-format banners (also: billboards, large leader-boards or mega banners)	Large advertising banners for special advertising placements (e.g., premium advertising spaces) Various sizes from 240 × 400 to 1024 × 768 pixels	Eye-catching banners with plenty of space for text and graphics	Due to their size, they can be perceived as a nuisance They can increase loading times due to their size
Small banners (also: button ads, micro bar, or badge)	Standard sizes include: 125 × 125 pixels (Button Ads) or 88 × 31 pixels (Micro Bar)	Lower costs and faster loading times due to the small size	Less visibility and fewer creative design options

Design and Placement

Several studies have investigated what influences the success of banner advertising. Arholdt et al. (2023) cite the results of several studies, the main findings of which can be summarized as follows:

1. **Content design.**

    - Targeting: Banner ads should be tailored to the interests and motivations of the target audience in order to achieve a higher click-through rate (CTR).
    - Congruence with site content: The ad content should be related to the content of the website on which the ad is placed.
    - Emotional appeal: Banners with emotional content (e.g., humor or eroticism) combined with purchase incentives can be more effective than purely rational banners.
    - Call to action: Discounts, free offers, or free shipping can increase the effectiveness of banner advertising.
    - Short messages: Messages that are too long or complex can have a negative impact on CTR.

- **Brand names**: The use of brand names can have varying effects. While well-known brands can achieve a higher CTR, non-branded ads can create curiosity and also have a positive impact on CTR.

2. **Graphic design.**
    - **Animation**: Animated banners can increase user attention and lead to higher click-through rates. They are also more memorable than static banners, especially when brand awareness and user experience are low.
    - **Appropriate level of animation**: Animations that are too fast or excessive can overwhelm the user's cognitive performance and make the advertising message unclear.

3. **Placement.**
    - **Personalized placement**: Personalized banner ad placement based on individual user profiles, as enabled by programmatic advertising, can increase ad effectiveness.

4. **Technological** aspects.
    - **Rich Media**: Technological developments such as plug-ins, JAVA script, GIF, Flash, and streaming media can be used to improve the design and interactivity of online banner ads.

2.3.4 Booking Advertising

2.3.4.1 Basic Advertising Booking Options

Booking is the process of buying and placing ads on selected platforms. In this step, the previously defined targeting parameters are applied to ensure that the ads are delivered to the right people. Different targeting options are available depending on the online environment or channels in which the ads are to be displayed (Sect. 2.3.2.2).

The options for booking online advertising can be structured as follows:

1. **Direct ad booking.**
   Here the booking is made directly with the provider/operator of a website, e.g.,

   - Website Operators & Publishers: Booking directly with website operators or publishers such as Spiegel Online, Zeit-Online.
   - Blogs: Posting on popular blogs such as TechCrunch, Mashable, t3n.
   - Social networks: Posting on platforms like Facebook, Instagram, LinkedIn, TikTok, Xing.
   - Online Retailers: Posting on e-commerce platforms like Amazon.
   - Mobile apps: include in-app advertising in games or news apps.
   - Comparison and review portals: Placement on platforms such as Check24 or Trustpilot.
   - Content aggregators: Placement on platforms such as Reddit or BuzzFeed.

2. **Online marketers.**
   Here, the booking is made through providers that have a large number of websites in their portfolio (Lammenett, 2021), e.g., Stroer Digital, Ad Alliance or Media Impact.

3. **Ad networks.**
   This is where ads are served through ad networks such as Google Display Network or Microsoft Audience Network, which serve ads across a large number of websites.

4. **Programmatic advertising.**
   Programmatic platforms (e.g., DoubleClick or AppNexus) are used here for automated, real-time ad buying based on specific audience and campaign parameters.

5. **Retargeting platforms.**
   Retargeting platforms such as AdRoll and Criteo are used to retarget users who have already interacted with the website or product.

Programmatic advertising is playing an increasingly important role in the booking and management of online advertising. In 2022, the global share of programmatic advertising was around 87% (PwC/iab, 2023).

Definition Programmatic advertising is an automated form of digital advertising in which the entire ad buying and placement process is controlled by the use of algorithms (Greve & Scheibe, 2020; Tischlinger, 2023; Mustapic, 2023).

Programmatic advertising enables the automated purchase of ad space in real time using a real-time bidding system. Advertising space is auctioned off individually and automatically in milliseconds, based on the advertiser's pre-defined criteria and bids, leading to enormous increases in efficiency. At the same time, however, advertisers always accept a certain loss of control as a result of automation (Greve & Scheibe, 2020; Mustapic, 2023).

Lammenett (2021) points out that programmatic advertising only becomes effective when a very large amount of data—and the associated high five- to six-figure advertising budgets—are available for automated optimization. As a result, programmatic advertising may not be suitable for smaller budgets.

One criticism of programmatic advertising is that it focuses on metrics such as click-through rates and impressions to increase efficiency. At the same time, the advertising environment in which the banner ad is placed has a major impact on the advertising impact. For example, it is recommended to place display ads on websites whose content matches the motives of the ad, as this can significantly increase the click-through rate, a phenomenon known as "context matching" (Arholdt et al., 2023). When planning and setting up display campaigns, it is therefore advisable to critically review the proposed website lists.

Quality criteria for the booking of advertising campaigns can be taken into account in the campaign settings.

2.3.4.2 Campaign Settings

The quality and effectiveness of online advertising campaigns depend heavily on the settings made beforehand. The following criteria are of central importance:

1. **Brand safety.**
    Brand safety concerns a key expectation of advertisers, namely the certainty that their ads will only be displayed in a brand-compliant environment (Johnson, et al., 2023). In order to avoid negative associations or brand damage. Impressions on sites that fall into one of the following eight key content categories are considered problematic adult content, alcohol, hate speech, illegal downloads, illegal drugs, offensive language, and controversial news and violence (IAS, 2022).
2. **Ad fraud.**
    Ad fraud is an illegal activity in digital advertising where individuals or organizations use deceptive methods to increase ad revenue or advertisers' costs. Common types include **placement fraud**, where ads appear on fraudulent or invisible sections of legitimate sites; **traffic fraud**, which uses bots or click farms to artificially inflate impressions or clicks; and **action fraud**, where fake user actions, like form submissions or online purchases, are generated to claim revenue (Sadeghpour & Vlajic, 2021).
3. **Visibility/viewability.**
    Viewability standards for online ads, as outlined in the MRC Viewable Ad Impression Measurement Guidelines, specify time and visibility requirements for ads to be counted as viewed. For display ads, at least 50% of an ad's pixels must be visible in the browser for one continuous second, with timing beginning only after the pixel criteria are met; strong user interactions, such as clicks, can override this time condition. For video ads, at least 50% of the pixels must be in view for two consecutive seconds, regardless of when the video begins, with user interactions also overriding time requirements (Media Rating Council, 2015). High ad viewability increases the likelihood that users will notice and interact with the ad.
4. **Frequency capping.**
    Advertisers can control ad display by setting a frequency cap, limiting the number of times an ad is shown to a user. This cap effectively prevents overexposure by ensuring the ad is only displayed until the cap is reached (Qin et al., 2015).

These settings can be made either directly through the platforms on which the campaigns are placed, or through additional tools and services from specialized third-party vendors such as Integral Ad Science, DoubleVerify, or AdSquirrel.

2.4 Step 3: Success Monitoring and Optimization

The success of each sub-campaign should be continuously monitored and optimized. The necessary steps are described in the following chapter.

2.4.1 Performance Measurement and Optimization

2.4.1.1 From Metrics to Key Performance Indicators: Measuring Success in Digital Marketing

Success measurement relies on the goals defined in the planning process, which each sub-campaign aims to achieve. It is helpful to distinguish between **raw metrics** (basic data), **key metrics** (evaluative indicators), and **Key Performance Indicators** (KPIs).

Definition Metrics are quantitative indicators that capture specific aspects or activities within a marketing campaign, such as the number of page views, time spent on a website, or bounce rate. These metrics provide raw data drawn directly from activities on the website, within the app, or across other digital channels. Typically unprocessed, they serve primarily as a foundation for deeper analysis.

Organizations have a variety of metrics that they can use to measure the success of their digital marketing efforts (Table 2.7).

Depending on the context and the specific objectives of the marketing activities, the listed metrics can function either as raw metrics or as key metrics.

Table 2.7 Digital marketing measurement metrics

Metric category	Explanation	Examples
Traffic metrics	Measure the number and type of visits to a website or app	Page views, unique visitors
Referrer metrics	Show from which external sources traffic comes to a website	Direct traffic, search engine traffic
Digital Ad metrics	Measure the effectiveness of digital advertising campaigns	Click-through rate (CTR), return on advertising spend (ROAS)
App metrics	Record the use and performance of a mobile application	App downloads, in-app purchases
Behavioral metrics	Record the behavior of users on a website or app	Dwell time, bounce rate
Device metrics	Provide information about which devices and operating systems are used by visitors	Mobile vs. desktop, operating system
SEO metrics	Measure the performance of a website in search engines	Organic search queries, keyword ranking
Social engagement metrics	Measure user interaction with content on social media	Likes and reactions, shares and retweets
Internal search metrics	Capture the behavior and efficiency of a website's internal search function	Search volume, exit rate after search
e-Commerce metrics	Measure the performance of an online store	Conversion rate, average shopping cart value
e-Payment metrics	Evaluate the efficiency and security of online payment processes	Aborted payments, successful transactions
Mailing & messaging Metrics	Measure the effectiveness of email and messaging campaigns	Open rate, click rate

1. **As raw metrics.**

   When these metrics are considered in isolation, without reference to overarching business or marketing objectives, they act as basic measurements. In this case, they provide raw quantitative data that describes user behavior or the performance of various elements of a website, application, or campaign.

2. **As key metrics.**
However, when these metrics are selected and specifically aligned to measure success against specific goals, they become key metrics. In this context, they provide an interpreted, goal-oriented view of the data that can be used for decision-making and strategy adjustments.

Example The Click-Through Rate (CTR) can serve as a simple metric for the number of clicks per ad impression. However, when it is selected as an indicator of campaign success in the context of increasing brand awareness, it becomes a key metric.

In management accounting, figures are considered key metrics if they quantitatively capture measurable facts in a concentrated form (Reichmann et al., 2017). But what distinguishes key metrics from Key Performance Indicators, or, in other words, when does a key metric become a KPI?

Definition Key Performance Indicators (KPIs) are those indicators that focus on the aspects of organizational performance that are the most critical for the current and future success of the organization. (Parmenter, 2019, p. 6).

Key Performance Indicators do not necessarily consist of a single metric. Depending on the objective being evaluated, it may be useful to combine multiple metrics to form a KPI. By combining different metrics, a KPI can be made more comprehensive and meaningful, which is advantageous for strategic analysis and decision-making processes.

Example An eBike manufacturer considers it a key success factor that potential customers spend as much time as possible on the website and engage with the company's products. The achievement of this objective is measured with the KPI "**User Engagement Score.**" The company proceeds as follows:

1. **Selection of measured variables.**
   The following metrics are considered relevant for calculating the user engagement score:

   - Bounce rate.
   - Average time spent on the page (Average Time on Page).
   - Average number of pages visited per session (Average Pages per Session).

2. **Weighting of the metrics.**
   As the individual metrics are classified as having different levels of importance for user engagement, the company weights them as follows:

   - Bounce rate: 40%.
   - Dwell time on the page: 30%.
   - Number of pages visited per session: 30%.

3. **Normalization of the metrics.**
   Since the metrics are measured in different units, normalization is necessary. A simple method of normalization is to convert each metric into a value between 0 and 1.
   The maximum <u>values</u> for normalization were defined by the company:

   - Maximum bounce rate: 100%.
   - Maximum dwell time: 10 min.
   - Maximum number of pages visited: 10.

   <u>Formula for the user engagement score.</u>
   The formula for the user engagement score for the company is as follows:

   $$\text{User Engagement Score} = (w1 * \text{Normalized Bounce Rate}) + \\ (w2 * \text{Normalized Avg Time on Page}) + \\ (w3 * \text{Normalized Avg Pages per Session})$$

   where $w1$, $w2$, and $w3$ are the weightings for the respective metrics.

4. **Calculation of the user engagement score.**
The company knows the following average values for visitor behavior on the website:

- Bounce rate = 50%.
- Dwell time on the page (Avg Time on Page) = 3 minutes.
- Pages visited per session (Avg Pages per Session) = 4.

This results in a **user engagement score of 41%** according to the following formula:

$$User\ Engagement\ Socre = \left(\begin{array}{c} (40\% * (1 - 50\%)) + \\ \left(30\% * \dfrac{3}{10}\right) + \left(30\% * \dfrac{4}{10}\right) \end{array} \right) = 41\%$$

In the ideal case (i.e., 0% bounce rate, 10 min average time on site, and 10 average pages viewed), the user engagement score would be 100%.

This score provides a holistic view of user engagement with the site. It can be monitored over time and compared to the scores of other sites to gain insight into the effectiveness of your own online efforts. The score also provides a basis for optimizing content and strategies to increase user engagement.

Companies have a wide range of metrics at their disposal to develop meaningful metrics, including from web analytics tools (e.g., Google Analytics), advertising platforms (e.g., Google Ads, Facebook Ads Manager), SEO tools (e.g., Semrush, Moz), e-commerce platforms (e.g., Shopify, Magento), and channel-specific tools (e.g., Mailchimp for email newsletters). From this flood of data, it is important to select the most appropriate data to monitor success. We will address this question in the next chapter.

2.4.1.2 Selecting Metrics for Performance Review

To maintain an overview and monitor the key metrics relevant for assessing and optimizing the success of online campaigns, we recommend organizing them as follows:

1. First, define one or more **primary KPIs** aligned with the overarching goal of the campaign to help assess goal achievement.
2. Define **additional key metrics** to evaluate **the efficiency of the activities**.
3. Select metrics and key metrics that **provide insights into user behavior**.

KPIs for the Awareness Phase

In the awareness phase, potential customers are at the beginning of their customer journey. This phase is characterized by a latent need, meaning customers are not yet actively searching for the product or information. During this phase, communication focuses on three objectives:

1. Increase brand awareness.
2. Arouse interest and latent needs of potential customers.
3. Encourage prospects to move to the next stage of the customer journey or to consider your company at this stage.

Display campaigns or social media campaigns, for example, can be used to achieve these goals. The following example illustrates which metrics can be used to measure success.

Example A company has developed innovative software for AI-based video creation. This generator can analyze text and produce high-quality videos in just a few minutes without the need for actors, cameras, or microphones. The target audience is primarily small businesses that want to create videos but do not want to hire outside companies to do so.

Table 2.8 Display campaign for the awareness phase

Customer needs	Latent, customer is not yet actively seeking for information
Marketing objectives in the awareness phase	Raise awareness of the company Create awareness of the new software Move customers to the next stage of the customer journey (here: ask stage, where customers gather information)

Campaign objective	Potential customers should
	  be exposed to the banner ad 4 times (reach & exposure; the company sets an exposure limit of 4 times)
	  visit the company's website (traffic)
	A visit to the website is a sign for the company that the next phase of the customer journey (ask phase) has been reached

Primary KPIs	The following KPIs can be used during the campaign period and at the end of the campaign to measure the success of the display campaign:
	1. Campaign objective "Reach & Contact Frequency"
	  (a) **Unique users** to measure the net reach
	  (b) Average **contact frequency**
	  (c) **Ad impressions** to measure gross reach
	2. Campaign Objective "Visit to homepage"
	  (d) Click-Through-Rate (CTR)

Key metrics for measuring efficiency	Advertising effectiveness can be measured using CPM (cost per mille)
Key metrics to better understand user behavior	These include **device metrics**, which provide information about what devices and operating systems users are using

The company believes that, unlike AI-powered text-to-speech software, only a small portion of the target audience is actively looking for such software. At the same time, however, discussions with potential customers show that there is a need for such solutions. The company therefore decides to launch an awareness campaign to raise its own company's profile through banner advertising (Table 2.8).

With regard to the campaign objective "visit to homepage," it is important to note that an evaluation based solely on CTR can provide an incomplete picture. A recent study by Wordstream shows that Google Ads will achieve an average CTR of 6.11% in 2023 (Irvine, 2024). In principle, however, contact with an ad can also encourage users to visit a company's website at a later date. This is known as post-view conversion.

KPIs for the Appeal Phase

The appeal phase is characterized by the fact that potential customers make a kind of "pre-selection" of the companies or brands they are interested in. In consumer behavior, we know the term "**evoked set**" (relevant set), which refers to a group of brands a consumer actively considers when making a purchase decision (Abougomaah, et al., 1987).

> **Important**
> A company that does not succeed in anchoring its own brand in the evoked set of potential customers will not be considered in the further purchase process.

The number of accepted brands from which the selection is made depends on the customer's previous experience with a product category, the basic interest, and the subjectively perceived purchase risk (Stankevich, 2017). Therefore, it is important for companies to anchor their own brand in the evoked set of potential customers. Communication at this stage therefore focuses on two objectives:

1. Communicating a clear brand image (what does the brand stand for?)
2. Gain the sympathy and trust of potential customers.

Content marketing or social media campaigns, for example, can be used to achieve these goals. The following example shows what metrics can be used to measure success.

Example The company from our previous example, which has developed AI-based video creation software, wants to launch an image campaign. The central idea of the campaign is to position the company as an innovator in the field of AI-based video creation and to emphasize the efficiency and quality of the software. The goal is to anchor the brand in the minds of the target audience and generate interest in the software.

The company chose the following tactics:

- **Video testimonials:**
    - (a) Authentic testimonials from satisfied customers demonstrating the benefits of AI-based video creation software.
    - (b) Channels: LinkedIn and YouTube.
- **Case Studies:**
    - (a) Detailed accounts of SMBs' successful use of the software, including challenges, solutions, and results.
    - (b) Channels: LinkedIn (Table 2.9).

KPIs for the Ask Phase

In the Ask phase, prospects are actively seeking information. The length and intensity of the search depends on the customer's level of engagement and varies widely by product category and industry. The possibilities range from "skipping" the ask phase (e.g., when they habitually reach for their favorite brand in the grocery store) to a very long ask phase with extensive lists of pros and cons (e.g., when buying real estate).

There are two main goals for communication at this stage:

1. Provide information that can be used to convince prospects of your offer.
2. To motivate potential customers to contact the company (e.g., to visit a branch or online store or to contact the sales department).

Table 2.9 Social media campaign for the appeal phase

Marketing objectives in the appeal phase	Communicate a clear brand image; position as an innovator Build trust in this type of video creation Encourage customers to consider the company in the next phase (here: ask phase, where customers get detailed information)

Campaign objective	The company is already active on LinkedIn, so the testimonial videos will be posted as organic posts and then promoted through the Sponsored Post feature. The case studies, which are available for download on the company's landing page, are also teased in the videos.
	The company chooses "website visits" as the campaign objective because the ad will be shown to people in the target audience who are most likely to click on the landing page.
	Potential customers should
	  be exposed to the videos (reach),
	  interact with the videos (clicks), and
	  download the case studies

Primary KPIs	The following KPIs can be used during the campaign and at the end of the campaign to measure the success of the campaign:
	1. Campaign Objective "Reach"
	  (a) **Impressions** to measure reach
	2. Campaign Objective "Interaction"
	  (b) Number of **clicks** and
	  (c) Click-through-rate (CTR)
	3. Downloads of the Cas-Study
	  (d) Number of **downloads** from the landing page

Key metrics for measuring efficiency	Advertising effectiveness can be measured using **CPM** (cost per mille) and **CPC** (cost per click).
Key metrics to better understand user behavior	LinkedIn provides a variety of demographic and job-related information about the people reached through sponsored content, including the job role, job title, company, industry, career level, size, work location, and country (LinkedIn, n.d.).

To achieve these goals, search engine advertising can be used in the form of search ads and display ads. The following example shows the metrics that can be used to measure success.

Example The maker of AI-based video creation software relies on search and display ads on Google in the "ask" phase of the customer journey. The goal of the campaign is to drive prospects to the company's landing page, where they can learn more about the company's offerings.

In contrast to the Awareness stage, where customers (still) have a latent need, customers in the Ask stage are already actively looking for information. For this reason, the company decides to take the following action:

- **Video Action Campaign on YouTube:**
  This is an automated campaign of skippable video ads designed to drive lower-funnel actions (e.g., website clicks). This type of campaign is designed to drive more conversions both on and off YouTube (Table 2.10).

Campaigns provide companies with information about the people who interacted with the ads through each channel. This knowledge can be used to further develop their own buyer personas.

2.4.2 Refining the Initial Buyer Persona

When planning online campaigns, the major digital players such as Google, Meta, TikTok, and LinkedIn offer extensive options for targeting relevant audiences. Not all of this information is available to analyze the users who have interacted with an online campaign. The focus is clearly on providing metrics that can be used to measure and continually optimize the success of the online campaign.

However, it also provides information about the audience that was actually reached, allowing you to learn more about your audience and develop your own buyer personas. The type and scope of the data differs depending on the provider.

- For **Google Display Ads**, Google Ad Manager provides information on the demographics of the people reached by the ad, including age, gender, household income, and parental status, with categories such as age ranges (18–24 to 65+), gender (Female, Male, Unknown), and income brackets (Top 10%, Lower 50%, etc.), though income targeting may not be available in all countries. Additionally, optional detailed demographics allow

Table 2.10 Online campaign in the ask phase

Marketing objectives in the ask phase	Communicate the key benefits of the product Drive potential customers to the company's online store to make a purchase
Campaign objective	The company wants to use the campaign to target potential customers who are already considering purchasing AI-powered video creation software. The video action campaign is designed to drive them to the company's online store where they can purchase the software. To measure the desired conversion—product purchase—conversion tracking must be set up on the website to measure what happened after the ad was clicked. Potential customers should interact with the videos (clicks) and buy the software in the online store (conversions)
Primary KPIs	The following KPIs can be used during the campaign and at the end of the campaign to measure the success of the campaign: 1. Campaign objective "Interaction" (a) Number of **clicks** and (b) **Click-through-rate** (CTR) 2. Campaign goal "Conversions" (c) Number of **product purchases** (d) **Conversion rate** (percentage of people who made a purchase) (e) Campaign return on investment (ROI)
Key metrics for measuring efficiency	Advertising effectiveness can be measured using **CPM** (cost per mille) and **CPV** (cost per conversion).
Key metrics to better understand user behavior	Google Ads offers a variety of reporting features and analytics that allow advertisers to learn more about the people who have interacted with their campaigns, including demographic and geographic data, interests and affinities, device data, and more.

more specific segmentation, such as targeting parents based on children's age groups, along with options for marital status, education, homeownership, and employment (Moons, 2022). By linking Google Ads with Google Analytics, you can view Google Analytics statistics in Google Ads and analyze Google Ads performance in Google Analytics.
- For **ads on LinkedIn**, extensive demographic and job-related information is available about the users reached by the ad (job role, job

title, company, industry, career level, size, location, and country) (Martin, 2024).
- **Meta** also provides comprehensive data for evaluating ads on Facebook and Instagram; demographic data (age, gender), geographic data (country, region, DMA region), and other data about the platform or time of day the ad was viewed are available for the people reached by an online campaign (Newberry & Lauron, 2023).
- **TikTok** also provides data on the demographics of the users reached (age, gender), geographic data (country, state), as well as the top 10 and bottom 10 interests and information on the device model and operating system used.

In the following chapters, we will show you how to implement your advertising campaigns in each of the digital channels.

References

Abougomaah, N. H., Schlacter, J. L., & Gaidis, W. (1987). Elimination and choice phases in evoked set formation. *Journal of Consumer Marketing, 4*(4), 67–72. https://doi.org/10.1108/eb008212

Akhoondnejad, A., Rosin, C., & Brennan, C. (2024). A new approach to understanding involvement: Linking involvement to the memorability of experience. *Journal of Marketing Analytics.* https://doi.org/10.1057/s41270-024-00295-1

Arholdt, D., Greve, G., & Hopf, G. (2023). *Online-marketing-intelligence: Erfolgsfaktoren, Kennzahlen und Steuerungskonzepte für praxisorientiertes digital-marketing* (2nd ed.). Springer Gabler.

Baxendale, S., Macdonald, E. K., & Wilson, H. N. (2015). The impact of different touchpoints on brand consideration. *Journal of Retailing, 91*(2), 235–253.

Blomkvist, S. (2002). Persona – An overview. In *The user as a personality: Using personas as a tool for design.* Position paper for the course workshop Theoretical perspectives in Human-Computer Interaction at IPLab, KTH, September 3, 2002.

BVWD. (2023, September 20). *OVK-Prognose für digitale Werbung 2023 – Umsätze auf Wachstumskurs.* Retrieved from https://www.bvdw.org/news-und-publikationen/ovk-prognose-fuer-digitale-werbung-2023-umsaetze-auf-wachstumskurs/

Christensen, C. M., Dillon, K., & Duncan, D. S. (2016, September). Know your customer's "jobs to be done". *Harvard Business Review*, 3–10.

Cooper, A. (1999). The inmates are running the asylum. In U. Arend, E. Eberleh, & K. Pitschke (Eds.), *Software-Ergonomie '99* (p. 53). Vieweg+Teubner Verlag. https://doi.org/10.1007/978-3-322-99786-9_1

Cooper, B., & Vlaskovits, P. (2013). *The lean entrepreneur: How visionaries create products, innovate with new ventures, and disrupt markets*. Wiley.

Czinkota, M. R., Kotabe, M., Vrontis, D., & Shams, S. M. R. (2021). *Marketing management: Past, present and future*. Springer. https://doi.org/10.1007/978-3-030-66916-4

Davis, M. (2005). Advertising planning and budgeting. In A. Mackay (Ed.), *The practice of advertising* (5th ed., pp. 173–189). Routledge.

Esch, F.-J., & Winter, K. (2009). Entwicklung von Kommunikationsstrategien. In M. Bruhn, F.-J. Esch, & T. Langner (Eds.), *Handbuch Kommunikation. Grundlagen – Innovative Ansätze – Praktische Umsetzung* (pp. 415–436). Gabler.

Fuchs, W., & Unger, F. (2014). *Management der Marketing-Kommunikation* (5th ed.). Springer Gabler.

Gaur, J., & Bharti, K. (2020). Attribution modelling in marketing: Literature review and research agenda. *Academy of Marketing Studies Journal, 24*(4), 1–21.

Google Ads Editor Help. (n.d.). *Image sizes for image ads*. Retrieved from https://support.google.com/google-ads/editor/answer/57755?hl=en#zippy=%2Cdisplay-ads%2Capp-ads%2Cvideo-ads%2Clocal-ads%2Cdiscovery-ads%2Cimage-assets

Google. (2022, August). *Mit YouTube effektiv Ihre Zielgruppe erreichen*. Retrieved from https://www.thinkwithgoogle.com/intl/de-de/marketing-strategien/video/youtube-mediadaten/

Greve, G., & Scheibe, M. (2020). Programmatic advertising – Möglichkeiten und Grenzen bei Display-Advertising am Beispiel hedonistischer und utilitaristischer Produkte. In S. Boßow-Thies, C. Hofmann-Stölting, & H. Jochims (Eds.), *Data-driven marketing*. Springer Gabler. https://doi.org/10.1007/978-3-658-29995-8_5

IAS. (2022). *Media quality report* (17th ed.). Retrieved from https://integralads.com/de/insider/media-quality-report-edition-17/

Irvine, M. (2024, May 13). *Google Ads benchmark for YOUR industry* (Updated!). Wordstream. [Online]. Available at: https://www.wordstream.com/blog/ws/2016/02/29/google-adwords-industry-benchmarks

Johnson, R., Voorhees, C. M., & Khodakarami, F. (2023). Is your brand protected? *Journal of Advertising Research, 63*, 205–220.

Jolaoso, C. (2023). What are display ads? Definition & best practices. *Forbes*. Retrieved from https://www.forbes.com/advisor/business/software/display-ads/

Kolsarici, C., Vakratsas, D., & Naik, P. A. (2020). The anatomy of the advertising budget decision: How analytics and heuristics drive sales performance. *Journal of Marketing Research, 57*(3), 468–488. https://doi.org/10.1177/0022243720907578

Kotler, P., Kartajaya, H., & Setiawan, I. (2017). *Marketing 4.0: Moving from traditional to digital*. Wiley.

Kotler, P., Keller, K. L., & Chernev, A. (2021). *Marketing management (global ed.)* (16th ed.). Pearson.

Kreutzer, R. (2023). *Practice-oriented marketing: Basics – Instruments – Case studies*. Springer Gabler.

Lammenett, E. (2021). *Praxiswissen online-marketing*. Springer Gabler. https://doi.org/10.1007/978-3-658-25135-2

Lischka, H., & Prohst, M. (2018). Dynamic pricing. In P. Kürble & H. Lischka (Eds.), *Trends und Forschung im Marketingmanagement* (pp. 143–172). De Gruyter.

Martin, M. (2024, February 21). *2024 LinkedIn demographics that matter to marketers*. Hootsuite. Retrieved from https://blog.hootsuite.com/linkedin-demographics-for-business/#How_to_pick_the_right_demographics_for_your_LinkedIn_ad_campaign

Media Rating Council. (2015). *MRC viewable ad impression measurement guidelines (desktop), version 2.0*. Media Rating Council. Retrieved from https://www.mediaratingcouncil.org/sites/default/files/Standards/081815%20Viewable%20Ad%20Impression%20Guideline_v2.0_Final.pdf

Michaelidou, N., & Dibb, S. (2008). Consumer involvement: A new perspective. *Marketing Review, 8*(1), 83–99.

Moons, D. (2022, October 10). *How to use Google Ads demographics to enhance your campaigns*. Store Growers. Retrieved from https://www.storegrowers.com/google-ads-demographics/

Mustapic, B. (2023, November 30). *Programmatic advertising*. SEMrush. https://www.semrush.com/blog/programmatic-advertising/

Newberry, C., & Lauron, S. (2023, April 6). *How to use Meta (Facebook) business manager: Complete guide*. Hootsuite. Retrieved from https://blog.hootsuite.com/facebook-business-manager-guide/

Osterwalder, A., Pigneuer, Y., Bernarda, G., Smith, A., & Papadakos, T. (2014). *Value proposition design: How to create products and services customers want*. Wiley.

Parmenter, D. (2019). *Key performance indicators: Developing, implementing, and using winning KPIs* (4th ed.). Wiley.

Percy, L., & Rosenbaum-Elliot. (2021). *Strategic advertising management* (6th ed.). Oxford University Press.

PwC/iab. (2023). *Internet advertising report: Full year 2022.* PwC & IAB. Retrieved from https://www.iab.com/insights/internet-advertising-revenue-report-full-year-2022/

Qin, R., Yuan, Y., Wang, F., & Li, J. (2015). Research on the frequency capping issue in RTB advertising: A computational experiment approach. In 2015 Chinese automation Congress (CAC) (pp. 258–263).

Reichmann, T., Kißler, M., & Baumöl, U. (2017). *Controlling mit Kennzahlen: Die systemgestützte Controlling-Funktion* (9th ed.). Vahlen.

Sadeghpour, S., & Vlajic, N. (2021). Ads and fraud: A comprehensive survey of fraud in online advertising. *Journal of Cybersecurity and Privacy, 1*(4), 804–832. https://doi.org/10.3390/jcp1040039

Sharma, R. (2023). *How does Google Ads generate responsive search ads?* PageTraffic. Retrieved from https://www.pagetraffic.com/blog/how-does-google-ads-generate-responsive-search-ads/

Smith, W. R. (1956). Product differentiation and market segmentation as alternative marketing strategies. *Journal of Marketing, 20*(3), 3–8.

Stankevich, A. (2017). Explaining the consumer decision-making process: Critical literature review. *Journal of International Business Research and Marketing, 2*(6), 7–14.

Statista. (2022a). *Statista-dossier DINKS (double income no kids) in Germany.* Statista. Retrieved from https://de.statista.com/statistik/studie/id/53001/dokument/dinks-in-deutschland/

Statista. (2022b). *Digital advertising – Market data analysis & forecast.* Statista. Retrieved from https://www.statista.com/study/42540/digital-advertising-report/

Tischlinger, D. (2023, August 22). *Programmatic advertising einfach erklärt.* HubSpot. Retrieved from https://blog.hubspot.de/marketing/programmatic-advertising

Vaclav, M. (n.d.). *Was sind buyer personas?* brandREACH. Retrieved from https://www.brandreach.at/blog/was-sind-buyer-personas

Vitale, R., Pfoertsch, W., & Giglierano, J. (2010). *Business to business marketing: Analysis and practice.* Pearson Prentice Hall.

Witell, L., Löfgren, M., & Dahlgaard, J. J. (2020). Empirical research on Kano's model and customer satisfaction. *Total Quality Management and Business Excellence, 24*(11–12), 1241–1252. https://doi.org/10.1080/14783363.2013.791117

3

Social Media Advertising

What You Will Take Away from This Chapter

- This chapter will provide an in-depth look at how companies can leverage social media for advertising purposes.
- We will explore the use of buyer personas as a tool for more efficient social media advertising, as well as methods for measuring the success of such campaigns.
- Finally, we will delve into the use of buyer personas for advertising on the most popular social media platforms.

3.1 Social Media in a Nutshell

The media and communication sector has changed dramatically over the past few decades. Today, social media in particular have a major influence on interpersonal communication and the overarching structures of media society—also or precisely because they include very different types of digitally networked communication. These include blogs, podcasts, wikis, and applications such as WhatsApp and Snapchat, but also websites and platforms such as Facebook, YouTube, Instagram, LinkedIn, TikTok, and X[1] (Wehrli et al., 2024). Internet-based social media are becoming an important means of accessing society and its surroundings and are replacing the once traditional mass media of radio, print media, and television. Online communication, like conventional mass media, has an enormous impact on social discussions because, in addition to providing information, these media also serve as a cultural memory, stimulate reflection, and offer an almost endless canvas for opinions, attitudes, and the exchange of experiences (Guetz & Bidmon, 2022a). The fundamental concept of social media is a new communication paradigm. In this context, a rough distinction can be made between one-to-many communication and many-to-many communication (de Moraes et al., 2007). In classic one-to-many communication, a sender (e.g., the initiator of a TV advertisement) communicates with a large number of recipients (e.g., the viewers). The many-to-many communication that characterizes social media is not as linear and directional as traditional forms of (advertising) communication (Gummesson, 2004). For example, if a company publishes a post on its own Facebook channel, followers of the company can view this post. However, mere viewing is not the only possible form of interaction with the post. Users have also the possibility to indicate which emotion they associate with the post (e.g., Like, Love, Hug, Haha, Wow, Sad, or Angry), comment on the post, and share its content.

The uniqueness of social media is emphasized by the ability to interact with other people within the network. This creates a link between mass media and interpersonal communication (Jensen, 2022). Consumers have the opportunity to create content and interact with companies and other users. The term user-generated content (UGC) is used for company-related content that is created by potential consumers. This type of content can be diverse and often goes beyond mere interaction with company content. In particular, this includes company or product reviews, but also all kinds of company-related content. Ideally, the content that is published by users about companies on social media creates a positive pull

---

[1] Formerly Twitter.

effect and thus actively supports corporate communication. It should be noted, however, that UGC can also include negative aspects. Negative posts are often spread even faster than positive posts about companies, which can lead to negative reputation in the worst case. Nevertheless, the generation and use of UGC is one of the great advantages of social media in the area of corporate communication (Müller & Christandl, 2019; Fink, 2021).

Social networks have rapidly developed into a user-intensive medium. While there were very few users 20 years ago, today more than half of the world's population is represented on social media. Although these platforms tended to be used by younger and tech-savvy target groups when they first emerged, it can now be assumed that the majority of the world population has the knowledge and ability to use social media (Auxier & Anderson 2021; Guetz & Bidmon 2022b; Appel et al., 2020a, b). In general, social media can be categorized into ten subgroups. These include *social networking platforms, video platforms, messenger services,* business *platforms, social* audio *platforms, blogs, micro blogs, forums* and *communities, content sharing platforms,* and *wikis* (Radcliffe, 2021):

- **Social networking platforms:** *Social networking platforms* are characterized by the fact that the focus is on the network of people. These include, e.g., Facebook, Instagram, and Snapchat (Arya et al., 2022).
- **Video platforms:** *Video platforms focus on* the consumption and distribution of video content. However, these portals also contain interaction functions and are often profile-based. The best-known *video platforms* on the Central European market include YouTube, TikTok, and Vimeo (Al-Maroof et al., 2021).
- **Messenger services:** In the area of *messenger services,* the focus is on interaction, which is usually text-based. As a rule, this interaction only takes place between two people at the same time. However, group interactions are also possible. The most widely used *messenger services* at present are WhatsApp, Facebook Messenger, and We Chat (Endeley, 2017).
- **Business platforms:** In contrast to the aforementioned social media, business *platforms* represent a newer category that are becoming increasingly popular, particularly within professional networking and

B2B marketing. The most used *business* platform worldwide is LinkedIn (Hoda et al., 2022).
- **Social audio platforms:** *Social audio* platforms are the newest category in the field of social media. These networks are characterized by the fact that interaction between users is mainly auditory, i.e., by means of voice and speech. The best-known *social audio* platform is Clubhouse. However, industry giants are already following suit with applications such as Facebook Live Audio Rooms or Spotify Greenroom (Zhu, 2021).
- **Blogs:** *Blogs* have also lost some of their satellite character and can now be published as part of various social media. Well-known social media *blogs* are Tumblr or Medium (Z).
- **Micro blogs:** In contrast to *blogs*, *micro* blogs have a limited number of characters. In this context, there is no way around the industry giant X. Nevertheless, it should be noted that there are also other *microblogging platforms* such as Plurk or Threads (Liu et al., 2020).
- **Forums and communities:** Users exchange information on specific topics in *forums* and *communities*. However, companies often also have the opportunity to create their own profiles in these online communities and participate in the discussions.
- **Content sharing platforms:** In addition to the social media platforms mentioned above, *content sharing platforms* are also becoming increasingly popular. Although these platforms are also about networking with one another, the focus is much more on sharing content than with the aforementioned portals. This content can be very diverse. While photos and videos are shared on Flickr, other platforms are mainly limited to static content. In contrast, documents can be shared online on the Scribd platform (Peng et al., 2018).
- **Wikis:** Finally, so-called *wikis are* also considered social media, as these portals are often profile-based and users have the possibility to interact with each other. The best-known *wiki* is Wikipedia. In recent years, however, other *wikis* have emerged that cover a variety of different topics. These include, for example, Mediawiki, TWiki, PmWiki, TikiWiki, and DokuWiki (Haidari et al., 2020).

Certain trends in the use of social media are particularly recognizable within younger target audiences. Behavior changes most rapidly within these groups and certain patterns of behavior can often be identified. There is currently a certain trend toward *live streaming platforms*. These platforms often have their origins in the gaming scene and make it possible to share interactions such as video games regardless of time and current location (Sheng & Kairam, 2020).

Another trend that is currently emerging is the desire for less loss of reality in the digital environment. After decades of heavily edited images in the media and advertising industry, this trend has continued with countless filtering and editing options on social media. The platform BeReal, for example, shows that the desire for realistic representations is growing. The platform, which is primarily aimed at Gen Z, enables real-time connectivity. Users only have two minutes to publish a post after receiving the daily notification. BeReal therefore attaches great importance to authenticity and contains neither filters nor editing tools (Boffon, 2022).

Despite the versatility and variation between different social media, these services still have some similarities in terms of their individual range of functionalities. For example, *timelines, communities, posts, bios, influencers, interaction options (reactions), news feeds,* and *user profiles* are available on almost all social media services (Fuchs, 2021):

- **Timelines:** A *timeline* is the profile page of a social media user. This consists of text, photo, and/or video posts by the user (Wong & Nguyen, 2021).
- **Communities:** A *community* is the group of people with whom private individuals are networked or who follow company profiles on social media (Papadopoulos et al., 2012).
- **Posts**: A *post* is a type of content that users of social media create and publish on the respective platform (Tafesse & Wien, 2017).
- **Bio:** The *bio*—short for biography—is the part of a social media profile in which personal data about social media users can be found (Wong, 2022).

- **Influencer:** An *influencer* is a medium that conveys communication content to decision-makers and even amplifies it. This interaction often takes place between people via social media (Vangelov, 2019).
- **Interactions(reactions):** Users on social media often have the opportunity to interact with content such as posts. Popular forms of interaction are likes, comments, or shared content (Huertas & Marine-Roig, 2016).
- **Newsfeeds:** In the context of social media, the term *newsfeed refers* to the area in which the latest information about subscribed or followed pages appears. The *newsfeed* is therefore the central point of contact for many social media platforms (Moniz & Torgo, 2018).
- **User profiles:** A *user profile* is a digital account operated by a person on social media. If a company is behind the account, it is usually a company profile which is operated by several individuals (Mezghani et al., 2015).

Within social networks interaction plays a crucial role for companies and individuals. When posts are created, the aim is for as many people as possible to see the post and even interact with it (Appel et al., 2020a, b). This interaction can take place, for example, by "liking," sharing or commenting on the post. Generally speaking:

> **Important**
> The more people connected or following a business page, the more likely people are to see the post.

This general basic rule applies equally to profiles of private individuals and company profiles (Lipsman et al., 2012). However, there are two other important aspects to consider in this context. On the one hand, not every person who sees a post interacts with it. The interaction itself depends on various factors such as the emotion that is triggered in the viewer, but also the situation in which the viewer currently finds him/herself. In addition, only a relatively small percentage of followers see the content, especially on company pages. In order to encourage companies to invest in advertising on social media, the organic reach[2] has been increasingly restricted in recent years. This means that it is becoming more and more difficult for companies to reach their potential customers without spending money for social media advertising (Chawla & Chodak, 2021). For this reason, small- and medium-sized companies are now also investing in advertising on social media. And it has already made a big splash. In the past, ROAS[3] values of several hundred percent have been generated with advertising on social networks (see e.g. Orzan et al., 2021).

3.2 Basic Procedure

Advertising on social media can be very successful. The major advantages of this advertising format include its versatility, cost transparency, and the fact that the attributes of the target group can be selected very precisely. Formats that can be used for online advertising include images, videos, surveys, infographics, and audio content. In addition to products, the company itself, and the online store, a variety of alternative online and offline content can be advertised. This includes e-books, studies, FAQs, mobile apps, webinars, newsletters, podcasts, blog articles, and tutorials. There are no limits to imagination in this context, although some of the content is editorially reviewed before publication (Jansasoy & Jansasoy, 2023).

The costs for advertising on social media can usually be monitored both within the platform and across all channels in real time. Views and interactions with the post, as well as the cost per click[4] of the respective

---

[2] The number of people on whose screens unpaid posts from a company page have appeared is referred to as "organic reach." This contrasts with the term "paid reach," which is used for posts that are generally shown to a significantly larger target group, as money has been paid to the operator of the social media platform for the increased reach (Pócs et al., 2021).

[3] Return on Ad Spend (ROAS) is a key figure that expresses how much profit an advertising campaign has generated compared to the costs of the campaign. ROAS = revenue ÷ advertising costs (*100 for %) (Moon et al., 2022).

[4] The cost-per-click (CPC) is a key figure that measures the costs incurred by an advertiser for a click on advertising content. For example, if the costs for a campaign are €100 and 10 people have clicked on the advertising content, the CPC is €10 (€100 (campaign costs)/10 (number of clicks = €10 (CPC)) (Hu et al., 2016).

campaign, are often available on the corporate dashboard provided by the operator of the respective platform. Applications such as Facebook Pixels[5] can also be used to track how page visitors reached the company website. This also enables control beyond the boundaries of the social media service (Iannelli et al., 2020). In contrast to traditional advertising formats, online advertising is generally characterized by the fact that the people who are supposed to see the ad can be filtered to a greater extent. However, this procedural approach only develops its efficiency when companies use social media. Users of these platforms spend many hours of their lives within these networks and willingly provide information about their wishes and current preferences through their profiles and interactions. In conjunction with demographic characteristics that users must enter in order to use the portals, this creates realistic digital personas of people who operate the respective profile. These personas can be actively addressed through online advertising on social media. Target groups can be segmented by location and age with almost all ad managers.[6] However, this only symbolizes the tip of the proverbial iceberg. With detailed targeting settings,[7] people can be targeted according to demographic characteristics such as education, relationship status or workplace, interests such as hobbies and activities and even based on their current behavior. It is therefore possible to target those social media users who, according to initial research or market research results, could have a general interest in the product or service. The segmentation categories are adapted to the respective groups of people. For example, the Facebook Ads Manager can be used to target people who have completed certain schools or courses

---

[5] The Facebook Pixel can link the actions of website visitors to their Facebook user accounts. It collects information that helps with the creation of target groups, the optimization of ads and the tracking of online user behavior (Bekos et al., 2022).

[6] Social media ad managers are powerful tools that allow companies to create, manage and optimize targeted advertising campaigns on platforms such as Facebook, Instagram, LinkedIn, YouTube, or TikTok. With these managers, advertisers can precisely define their target groups based on users' demographics, interests, behavior and even location. This makes it possible to maximize the effectiveness of ads and use the budget efficiently. The integrated analysis tools make it possible to monitor and adjust the success of campaigns in real time in order to achieve better results (Boffone, 2022).

[7] In social media marketing, targeting settings refer to the individual target group attributes. For example, users' profile data can be used to address a target group that is male, between 35 and 39 years old and has a particular preference for technical aspects of renewable energy (Jacobson et al., 2020).

of study, have a certain income,[8] have just got engaged or married, or have a birthday or other anniversary coming up soon. These target group attributes already give an initial indication that the target group is more likely to consist of private individuals. In contrast, the LinkedIn Campaign Manager is much more focused on the business-to-business sector. For example, you can categorize your audience by industry, turnover or company size.

Despite the many differences in terms of design elements, target groups, and functions, it is clear that social media and their ad managers are structured quite similarly in terms of their general operating elements. Just as *chronicles, interactions,* and *user profiles* are available for almost all social media services, most social media ad managers are characterized by the *selection of a project goal*, a certain *ad format*, an *ad preview*, the *selection of target group and persona,* the *duration,* a *daily budget,* the *result estimate,* and the *payment summary.*

- **Selection of a project goal:** An important principle of social media marketing is the *selection of a project goal*, which influences both the individual posts and campaigns as well as the overall plan. Content sharing is the lifeblood of social networks, so content that is intriguing, distinctive, and shareable is crucial. The term "social" should be taken seriously in this context and the marketing plan should address the social components of social media platforms. In order to be able to apply the *selection of a project goal,* to the respective campaign, social media ad managers offer a separate area for entering the *project goal*. Depending on the platform, this can be defined at macro or micro level. At the macro level, for example, *project goals* such as building brand awareness or creating interest in the product can be defined. At the micro level, the focus is often on functions that affect the platform itself. This includes the growth of the community, but also interactions with posts.
- **Ad format:** The *ad format* describes the form in which the ad is displayed. This varies between individual providers and ranges from static

---

[8] Currently only possible in the USA.

text or image ads (e.g., images, texts, or infographics) to moving images (animations or videos).
- **Ad preview:** The *ad preview* is available with most ad managers and allows the user to see what the published ad could look like while creating the ad.
- **Selection of target group and persona:** The core of the ad manager on social media is the *selection of target group and persona*. In this area, you can specify which gender the persona should belong to, which age group they are in, as well as their interests, preferences, and behavioral patterns.
- **Duration:** The *duration* of advertising campaigns can usually be limited. However, in most cases it is also possible to let the campaign run indefinitely for the time being and to stop or change it if necessary by intervening on the platform.
- **Daily budget:** The *daily budget* determines how much budget is available per day for the distribution of the campaign within the target group. It is often accepted in the terms of use that the daily *budget* may be exceeded or undercut by a certain percentage. Over a longer campaign period, however, these budget peaks usually balance each other out.
- **Result estimate:** The *result estimate* provides a rough indication of the reach and interactions that can be achieved with the publication of the campaign.
- **Payment summary:** The *payment summary* is presented in this section in a similar way and often in connection with the *results estimate*.
- **Platform-specific elements:** Depending on the target group and design of the respective social media platform, links to websites and online services or other social media and advertising platforms are set up in addition to the general operating elements in this area.

The successful creation of online advertising on social media requires a deep understanding of your target group. For this reason, buyer personas are essential, especially in the field of social media advertising. How you should generally proceed when creating buyer personas is explained in detail in Chap. 2. However, in order to be able to use them successfully in the social media environment, a predefined process should be followed. However, it is important to emphasize that the process for using buyer personas for online advertising on social media can vary depending on the company, industry, and target group. Every company has unique needs and challenges that require customization. Nevertheless, a typical process can serve as a point of reference. Below we outline the general process that can be used as guidance for creating personalized online advertising using buyer personas on social media. This process can be adapted and expanded to meet the specific needs of your business.

Step 1: The Definition of Buyer Personas
Before you can create your social media advertising, you need to create or revise your buyer personas. This step involves researching and analyzing your target audience to better understand their needs, challenges, behaviors, and preferences. You can use customer surveys, data analysis, and other market research tools to gather in-depth information. This data will help you to create detailed buyer personas that represent different segments of your target group.

Step 2: Selecting the Right Social Media
Not all social media are equally relevant for every buyer persona. Different platforms attract different target groups. Therefore, it is crucial to choose the right social media to reach your target groups effectively. For example, LinkedIn may be more effective for B2B personas, while Instagram is better suited for B2C personas. Careful analysis and selection of platforms is essential. Once you have selected the right platform(s), familiarize yourself with the ad manager of the respective platform. Ask yourself the following questions when selecting the platform(s):

1. Does my buyer persona use this platform?
2. Is it possible to achieve my (advertising) goal by displaying ads on this platform?
3. Is this platform suitable for spreading my (advertising) message?
4. Is my buyer persona on this platform receptive to my (advertising) message?

If the answer to these four questions is "yes," the platform is generally suitable for your online advertising.

Step 3: Enrichment of the Buyer Persona with Data from Social Media Advertising Managers

In the world of digital marketing, social media ad managers offer an impressive range of settings and characteristics that allow companies to create highly targeted advertising campaigns. However, this multi-faceted approach requires precise customization to the characteristics and objectives of each individual platform. The differences between platforms are striking and it is crucial to enrich the outlined persona with the specific criteria of each platform. A look at Facebook and LinkedIn shows how different audiences and marketing objectives can be reached by clever use of the tools:

- Facebook offers an enormous reach and is particularly suitable for brands that aim to increase their brand awareness and interact with a broad target group. Advertisers can use settings to select users based on their age, gender, location, and interests. For example, a fashion company targeting young adults in major cities could design the settings so that the ads appear in the feeds of people between the ages of 18 and 35 in metropolitan areas who have expressed an interest in fashion and lifestyle. Characteristics such as image or video advertising can be used to provide visually appealing content and capture the attention of the target audience.
- LinkedIn, on the other hand, is the ideal choice for companies that focus on B2B marketing and professional networking. The settings allow ads to be targeted by industry, company size, job titles, and user skills. For example, assuming an enterprise software provider wants to reach decision-makers in medium to large technology companies, they could target their ads to IT managers, CTOs, and CEOs in companies with more than 500 employees. LinkedIn ads can include informative articles, case studies, or whitepapers to engage the target audience with high-quality content.

Overall, this review highlights the importance of understanding the unique characteristics and target audiences of each social media platform and utilizing the settings and characteristics of each ad manager accordingly to create an effective social media advertising campaign. Careful customization to the platform is the only way to ensure that the ad reaches the right audience and achieves the desired marketing objectives. In this crucial phase, it is essential to continuously enrich and expand the outlined buyer persona with the information from the respective ad manager. The diverse data collected through the interactions and behavior of the target group on the platforms provides valuable insights into preferences, needs, and habits of potential customers. These insights enable companies to continuously optimize their advertising strategies and develop even more targeted campaigns in order to achieve sustainable engagement with the target group and ultimately increase the success of their social media marketing efforts. Continuously adapting and expanding the buyer persona is therefore the key to effective and targeted advertising in the ever-evolving world of social media.

Step 4: Content Creation for Buyer Personas
Once your buyer personas are defined, it's important to create targeted content that is tailored to each persona's platform, needs, and interests. This can include images, text, blog posts, videos, infographics, and more. Each persona should receive a customized content strategy that addresses their specific concerns and challenges. The content should be informative, relevant, and engaging to pique the interest of your target audience.

Step 5: Continuous Monitoring and Optimization
Creating online advertising with buyer personas is an ongoing process. Monitor the performance of your ads on the selected social media platforms. Analyze metrics such as the click through rate, the conversion rate, and the engagement rate.[9] Based on the results, you should regularly optimize and adjust your strategy. This can include fine-tuning ad copy, adjusting budget allocation, but also adapting, developing, or even revising your buyer personas.

---

[9] See Sect. 3.3 Measuring success on social media.

Creating online advertising with buyer personas on social media allows you to use personalization options efficiently in your marketing strategy. By targeting the specific needs and interests of your audience, you increase the relevance of your ads and maximize your chances of success. This process takes time, research, and continuous adjustments, but investing in personalized online advertising pays off in the long run and strengthens customer loyalty and the growth of your business.

3.3 Measuring Success on Social Media

Measuring success on social media makes it possible to monitor activities and evaluate the effectiveness of advertising campaigns. Continuous monitoring and refinement of campaigns also provides valuable insights into target behavior. When it comes to measuring success on social media, a distinction is made between general and advanced metrics or key performance indicators. The general metrics include *reach, engagement rate, conversion rate,* and *click through rate. Reach* is of fundamental importance when it comes to measuring success on social media. It shows how many people have seen certain posts, both organic and paid. *Engagement rate* plays a crucial role in assessing the response to social media content. Engagement metrics, which include likes, comments, forwards, or shares of content and clicks, provide important indications of how well content is received by the target group. Increased engagement indicates that content is relevant and appealing to the target group. The *conversion rate* measures how many users have carried out a desired action after viewing the post or ad, such as filling out a contact form or purchasing a product. This makes the *conversion rate* one of the most important metrics for assessing business success (Reddy et al., 2023). The *click through rate* is used to measure the relationship between the number of clicks on a social media post and the number of impressions of this post. It is usually expressed as a percentage and is used to evaluate the effectiveness of social media campaigns and other digital marketing activities (Yang & Zhai, 2022).

Advanced metrics or key figures include *conversion attribution* or *customer lifetime value. Conversion attribution makes it possible* to analyze the influence of different marketing measures. For example, it is possible to track whether an ad has contributed to customers buying a certain product, even if the purchase was made some time after clicking on the ad (Fetissova, 2022). *Customer lifetime value* is a metric that can be used to calculate the estimated value of customers over the entire duration of their customer relationship. This metric is crucial for determining how profitable social media campaigns are in the long term (Hofmann & Mertiens, 2012).

In addition to general and advanced metrics and key figures, social media dashboards are also important when it comes to measuring success on social media. Tools such as Facebook Insights or Instagram Insights provide detailed insights into company performance on these platforms. They enable the monitoring of key figures such as follower growth, reach, and target group demographics (Jadczak, 2023). Another important aspect of measuring success on social media is A/B testing. These tests make it possible to compare different ad variants or content to find out which works best. Different images, texts, target groups, or publication times can be tested in order to continuously optimize the strategy (Garrity, 2022).

Measuring success on social media is crucial to ensure that marketing activities are effective. By using appropriate metrics and applying advanced analytics techniques, strategy improvements, cost reductions, and maximizing ROI can be achieved. Especially in the social media space, it is crucial to stay informed of platform changes and adjust measurements to ensure continued success.

3.4 Application on Selected Channels

Over the past 10 years, the number of social media users worldwide has increased by more than 300%. While "only" 1.48 billion people worldwide had profiles on social media in 2012, this figure had risen to 5.17 billion by 2024 (Petrosyan, 2024). This shows that the use of these portals has increased significantly and is due to various underlying conditions. These include the advancing digitalization, but also the decreasing price level of devices that can be used to access social media (Bouwman et al., 2017). Excluding messaging services such as WhatsApp or WeChat, the most used social media services in 2024 include Facebook, YouTube, Instagram, and TikTok. Facebook is in first place with over 3 billion monthly active users. It is followed by the video platform YouTube with 2.5 billion monthly active users and the video and photo sharing network Instagram with 2 billion users. The rising star in the social media sector is TikTok, a provider specializing in short videos, with around 1.6 billion monthly active users (Bernhardt, 2024). In line with this ranking, the next chapters will present the social media services with the highest reach, their ad managers, and the use of buyer personas for social media advertising.

3.4.1 Facebook and Instagram

3.4.1.1 Characteristics of Facebook and Instagram

As an integrated platform, Facebook offers users access to multiple applications after registration. The most important function is a constantly updated *timeline* in which users can read posts from Facebook contacts and comment on or rate them (e.g., with a "Like"). These posts are selected on the basis of users' preferences and their previous usage habits on the platform using dynamic algorithmic filtering and ranking mechanisms. Accordingly, users' perceptions vary depending on the situation and they are not aware of how their perceptions are influenced or controlled. Facebook also offers a wide range of coordination and communication options, from private discussions, public or private discussion groups, and fan pages to countless opportunities for socializing and self-expression (Marshall et al., 2020).

While Facebook is characterized by a variety of different format options, Instagram focuses on sharing photos and videos. In contrast to Facebook, Instagram was initially characterized by the ability to add filters to the photos and videos to be shared. The platform is still referred as a network of images. Like Facebook, Instagram offers a *timeline* where any user has the possibility to post content. As well as uploading your own content, Instagram as a community thrives on comments, likes and following or subscribing to other people or businesses (Basit et al., 2020).

3.4.1.2 Campaign Settings on Facebook and Instagram

In addition to a personal account, a company account can also be created on both Facebook and Instagram. Among other things, this company account also offers the option of transporting content directly to people from the selected target group. As Facebook and Instagram are both part of the Meta Group, joint advertisements (advertising via Facebook and Instagram) can be created using the Facebook Ads Manager. Ad management on Facebook can be roughly divided into two categories. Firstly, there is traditional *post promotion,* in which the shared post on Facebook and/or Instagram is made accessible to a wider audience. It is also possible to place ads that are created individually and do not have to be published as content on the corresponding company page (Gebel, 2020). The following overview summarizes the areas of *selection of a project goal, ad format, ad preview, selection of target group and persona, duration, daily budget, result estimate, payment summary,* and *platform-specific elements* of the Facebook ad manager:

- **Selection of a project goal:** The default setting in the Facebook Ads Manager is set to *Automatic.* If this setting is retained, Facebook selects the most relevant objective based on the settings selected. The possible goals in this category are *Get more calls,* Get *more website visitors, Get more messages, Get more Page likes, Get more visits,* or *Get more leads.* With the *project goal Get more calls,* social media ads are displayed to people who are likely to call the company. The more *website visitors* objective shows the ad mainly to people who are likely to click on the link embedded in the ad. People who are likely to send the company a message (e.g., an inquiry) via the platform are reached with the target project *Get more messages.* The target project *Get more Page likes* is used so that more people find the company page and mark it with a "like." *Get more visits* shows the ad to people who are likely to visit the companies social media page. With the *project goal Get more leads,* a

form is created with which the contact information of potential customers can be recorded.
- **Ad format:** Within the Facebook Ads Manager ads generally consist of a *headline*, a *description,* the *media (*image or a video), the *button label* (this button contains the link), and the *info labels.* The *headline* and the *description* can be freely selected. For the *media,* either a static graphic (e.g., photo or infographic) or a moving image (e.g., company video) must be selected. In order to create a carousel (several contents that can be pushed forward), it is also possible to upload several images or videos. The possible *button labeling* is very diverse. You can choose between the following buttons: "Like page," "Send message," "Send WhatsApp message," "Call now," "Apply now," "Book now," "Contact us," "Download," "Learn more," "Request time," "See menu," "Shop now," "Sign up," "Watch more," "Donate now," "Get quote," "Subscribe," or "Visit Page." Depending on the *button label* selected, it may be necessary to enter further information (e.g., telephone number).
- **Ad preview:** The *ad preview* is located at the top right during the entire creation process and actively evolves depending on the selected setting. By clicking on the "See all previews" button, you have the option of accessing various previews of possible Facebook ads, Instagram ads, Facebook Messenger ads, and Audience Network.
- **Selection of target group and persona:** The *target group and persona* are selected via audiences. In addition to the rather general target groups "People who like your page" and "People who like your page and similar people," it is also possible to define your own target group or persona. The first step is to define the gender (male/female) of the target group and the age group (possible from 13–65+ years). In addition, the location of the target group can be entered down to a radius of one kilometer. Detailed targeting options are also available in within the categories of demographics, interests, and behaviors. In the demographics category, the people who are to see the ad can be segmented according to education, finances, life events, parents, relationship, and work. In terms of interests, the preferences of viewers can be predefined with regard to business and industry, entertainment, family and relationships, fitness and wellness, food and drink, hobbies and activities as well as shopping and fashion. In the area of behaviors, criteria can

also be defined with regard to anniversaries, mobile device users, consumer classification, digital activities, and expands.

- **Duration:** The duration can be defined continuously within the Facebook Ads Manager or based on duration days or end date. The default setting is a runtime of 7 days.
- **Daily budget:** The daily budget determines how much you are prepared to spend on the campaign in 1 day. Increasing the budget also increases the reach.
- **Result estimate:** The result estimate predicts both the estimated reach—i.e., how many people can generally be reached with the ad—and the expected link clicks.
- **Presentation of the expected costs:** The presentation of the expected costs includes the daily budget as well as the total budget and the total amount expected to be paid.
- **Platform-specific elements:** A special feature of Facebook Ads Manager is that ads can not only be designed for Facebook itself, but can also be played out directly on Instagram, via Facebook Messenger and Audience Network. To run effective advertising campaigns on Facebook and Instagram, it is crucial that you know your buyer personas well. This includes demographic information such as age, gender, profession, and income, but also psychographic characteristics such as interests, values, and purchasing behavior. The more detailed and accurate you can define your buyer personas, the better you will be able to customize your advertising message and appeal to your target audience. Facebook and Instagram offer a variety of audience segmentation options, including demographics, geographic locations, interests, behaviors, and more. By matching your buyer personas with these segmentation options, you can ensure that your ads are only seen by those who are most likely to be interested in your product or service.

Creating ads that are tailored to your buyer personas is crucial to the success of your social media advertising campaigns. Remember that your ads should not look like advertising, but rather valuable content that meets the needs and interests of your target audience. The final step in creating social media ads on Facebook and Instagram with buyer personas is to continuously monitor and optimize your campaigns. Use the analytics tools available on these platforms to track the performance of your ads. Pay attention to metrics such as reach, engagement rate, conversion rate, and click through rate. If you find that your ads are not achieving the desired results, make adjustments. This could include adjusting your buyer persona, changing ad content, or adjusting your budget.

Using buyer personas in your social media advertising on Facebook and Instagram can make a significant difference in the effectiveness of your campaigns. By better understanding and targeting your audience, you can optimize your ad spend and achieve better results. Remember that the process of creating and optimizing ad campaigns is continuous and you should always be experimenting to find out what works best.

3.4.2 LinkedIn

3.4.2.1 Characteristics of LinkedIn

Similar to Facebook and Instagram in B2C marketing, LinkedIn has also developed into one of the most important marketing tools for the B2B sector in recent years. B2B marketing is also becoming increasingly digital. New business relationships are facilitated by digital communication. It has never been easier to speak openly and at eye level with potential customers, industry professionals, and experts to discuss and launch joint projects. Corporate social networks, such as LinkedIn, play a major role as information hubs and meeting places for the digital sector. They also offer the opportunity to improve your own positioning and public image while being perceived as an industry professional. This makes it possible to be noticed by potential customers and business partners and opens the door to developing new business relationships (Macarthy, 2021).

With over 1 billion members worldwide, the business network LinkedIn has become the most important social network for the B2B sector (Shepherd, 2024). In fact, one gets the impression that many opinion leaders who previously shared their day-to-day professional activities on other social media platforms are now present on LinkedIn. However, the focus within the business network is different, because unlike alternative social media platforms, LinkedIn is more about business than personal life. You make contacts, maintain and sharpen your own profile or that of your company or brand. Companies can also create profiles, publish organic and paid posts, and recruit new employees. In marketing, LinkedIn has therefore become an important platform for building and strengthening the brand image, but also in the area of content marketing and online advertising (Gebel, 2020).

3.4.2.2 Campaign Settings on LinkedIn

LinkedIn allows you to create both personal and business accounts, just like Facebook and Instagram. By using a company account, access to the LinkedIn Campaign Manager is activated. The LinkedIn Campaign Manager is the advertising platform for the company's marketing on the business network. This is where the goals and target markets are defined, the ads are designed and the campaigns are tracked and improved (LinkedIn, 2022). The following overview summarizes the areas of *campaign objective, ad format, ad preview, selection of target group and persona, duration, daily budget, result estimate, payment summary,* and *platform-specific elements* of the LinkedIn Campaign Manager:

- **Campaign objective:** The *campaign objective* is divided into three main categories and nine subcategories. The main categories are "Awareness," "Consideration," and "Conversions." Within the "Awareness" category, the sub-target "Brand Awareness" can be selected. The aim of "Brand Awareness" is to increase brand awareness through the ad. In the Consideration area, the sub-targets "Website visits," "Engagement," "Video views," or "Messaging" can be selected. The "Website visits" objective is intended to encourage users to click on the link in the ad and visit the website. By selecting the campaign objective "Engagement," the ad is displayed to those people who are most likely to respond to the ad or follow the company. If, on the other hand, the campaign objective "Video views" is selected, the ad is shown to those people who are most likely to watch the uploaded video. "Messaging" increases engagement with the audience through messaging. Four more sub-targets are included within the main category "Conversions." You can choose between the subcategory "Lead generation," "Talent leads," "Website conversions," and "Job applicants." The Lead Generation sub-target shows the ad to people who are most likely to fill out a LinkedIn Lead Gen form. The campaign objective "Talent leads" results in the most promising group of people being shown the ad for interested candidates, which increases the likelihood that the post will be viewed or clicked.[10] If the campaign objective is "Website conversions", the ad will be shown to the people most likely to take the actions previously defined as useful to the business. Finally, the sub-target "Job applications" results in the ad being displayed to people who are most likely to view or click on the job ad.

- **Ad format:** The following nine formats are available in the LinkedIn Campaign Manager: "Single Image Ad," "Carousel Image Ad," "Video Ad," "Text Ad," "Spotlight Ad," "Follower Ad," "Document Ad," "Conversion Ad," and "Event Ad." Selecting "Single Image Ad" creates a newsfeed ad with a single image. The "Carousel Image Ad" consists of two or more images that appear in the newsfeed. Selecting "Video Ad" creates newsfeed ads with a video. The "Text Ad" creates text ads that appear on the LinkedIn page in the right-hand column or at the top. "Spotlight Ads" and "Follower Ads" use members' profile data to advertise a specific offer on the LinkedIn desktop page. By selecting "Document Ad," documents, slides, instructions, or ads can be created for the LinkedIn feed. Selecting "Conversation Ad" creates ads that are delivered to the target group via the LinkedIn inbox. Selecting "Event Ad" creates an event announcement that is displayed in the LinkedIn feed of the selected target group.
- **Ad preview:** Unlike the Facebook and Instagram Ads Manager, the LinkedIn Campaign Manager does not offer a continuous *ad preview*. Although the format is predefined in the first step, the ad itself can only be created and reviewed in the second step. Here you have the option to create a new ad or to browse through the content that is already available.

---

[10] The LinkedIn Recruiter add-on is required to select this campaign objective.

- **Selection of target group and persona:** To *select the target group and persona*, the current or permanent location of the target group is primarily available for selection. This can be narrowed down to city level (e.g., London, Singapore, or New York). If a certain region has too few LinkedIn members, the target group is too small to start an ad campaign and additional regions must be specified. There are no restrictions at country level (e.g., England, China, or the USA) or continental level (e.g., Europe, Africa, or North America). A special feature of the target group selection on LinkedIn is that it is also possible to exclude people from certain regions. This exclusion can in turn be made at city, country, or even continental level. In the second step, the profile language—i.e., the language in which members use their LinkedIn account—is selected. Within the detailed selection of the target group, existing data can be used to retarget[11] people who have already visited the company's website or have had a relationship with the company or third-party providers in some other way. In addition to the option of using existing customer data to define the target group, it is also possible to define the persona using different target group attributes. The main categories in this area are "Company," "Demographics," "Education," "Job Experience," and "Interests and Traits." In the main category "Company," you can select the industries in which the persona should be active, how high the company's annual turnover should be, whether the persona follows the advertiser company, how large the company is, which contacts are networked with the company and how high the company's annual growth should be. The age group and gender of the persona can be defined within the main category of "Demographics." The main category "Education" gives users the option of segmenting ad recipients based on degrees (e.g., Dr. phil., M.A., Bachelor, professional diploma or Master), universities (e.g., Oxford, Stanford, University of Vienna or ETH Zurich), or fields of study (e.g., economics, social sciences, computer science, marketing, or business management). The main category "Job experience" enables

---

[11] Retargeting is a common variant of behavior-based advertising that uses the online behavior of users on websites to reach those users again, encourage them to visit the website again, and ultimately make a purchase.

target groups and personas to be selected based on job functions, job stages, member skills, and years of experience. Within the main category "Interests and traits," group affiliations, general interests, and product interests as well as characteristics of the LinkedIn members who should see the ad can be defined. Linkedin members can also be excluded based on target group attributes.
- **Duration:** The campaign duration setting can be found in the LinkedIn Campaign Manager within the Schedule category. Here you can choose between continuous execution of the campaign and a runtime with a start and end date.
- **Daily budget:** The campaign budget can be set within the LinkedIn Campaign Manager as a *daily budget* or *lifetime budget*.
- **Result estimation:** The *result estimation* is highly target group-specific. When entering various target group attributes, the size of the target group is adjusted accordingly. It is also possible to display the Segment breakdown according to the selected segmentation criteria. This detailed forecast is followed by a result estimate of the impressions, clicks, and click through rate.
- **Payment summary:** The *payment summary* is shown as a cost estimate for the selected duration and as costs per click. If no end date is selected for the publication of the campaign, the cost blocks can be forecast for 1, 7, or 30 days.
- **Platform-specific elements:** The LinkedIn Campaign Manager offers some special features. By using the included LinkedIn Audience Network, ads can be placed on third-party publishing platforms where LinkedIn target groups are active. In addition, the conversion tracking option can be used to measure which actions visitors take on the respective company website or landing page after they have clicked on the LinkedIn ad. Finally, LinkedIn also offers a number of pre-defined target groups (e.g., members with a bachelor's degree or with expertise in development activities) that can be selected without having to pre-define individual target group attributes.

Before you start your LinkedIn advertising campaigns, you need to create your buyer personas and enrich them with data from the LinkedIn Ads Manager as described in Sect. 3.2. Once you have developed your

LinkedIn buyer personas, you can create your advertising campaigns. LinkedIn offers a variety of advertising options. Choosing the right format depends on your goals and the buyer personas you want to target. In addition to choosing the right format, you can segment your target groups on LinkedIn. As with any advertising campaign, it's crucial to monitor the performance of your LinkedIn ads and optimize them as needed. Pay attention to metrics such as reach, engagement rate, conversion rate, and click through rate. Adjust your ads, persona, or budget to achieve better results.

LinkedIn offers a unique platform for B2B advertising and business development. By using buyer personas, you can tailor your advertising campaigns to your target audience and significantly improve your chances of success. Make sure your ads and content are professional and relevant, and continuously optimize your campaigns to get the best results.

3.4.3 YouTube

3.4.3.1 Characteristics of YouTube

YouTube is one of the most important platforms for the distribution of videos. Founded in 2005, the content community enables users to publish, view, comment on, and share a variety of content (Dehghani et al., 2016). Although the social media service has become the largest video platform in the world today, the importance of YouTube as a social media network is often underestimated. Yet the platform is ideally suited for the successful development of online marketing and customer communication strategies. Small and medium-sized enterprises, freelancers, and artists all have the potential to use YouTube for effective online marketing, significantly increase their brand awareness and ultimately operate much more successfully on the market (Febriyantoro, 2020). Companies have the opportunity to observe customer behavior and communicate with people on YouTube. With this approach, the efficiency of advertising can be measured not only by the number of views, but also by likes, dislikes, and comments. The environment therefore offers ideal conditions for measuring online advertising effectiveness. Understanding the success criteria of advertising remains important due to the growing pressure of advertising on social media. While most companies already measure the success of their social media activities, they continue to conduct traditional survey-based advertising performance studies in parallel. This approach offers the opportunity to document the long-term impact of advertising and provide an explanation for success or failure by identifying variations in advertising content. However, the three factors of authenticity, innovation, and interactivity are crucial for the success of YouTube videos. While the prerequisites for each of these three characteristics are already created during the production of a video, interactive components can be added, expanded, or removed at any point in the finished product, depending on the goals of the viewers (Belanche et al., 2020).

3.4.3.2 Campaign Settings on YouTube

As with Facebook, Instagram, and LinkedIn, both personal and business accounts can be created on YouTube. Video ads can generally be created for both types of accounts. As YouTube has been part of the Google Group since 2006, advertising is managed via Google Ads. The following overview summarizes the areas of *selecting a project goal & ad format*, the *ad preview*, the *selection of target group and persona*, the *duration*, the *daily budget*, the *result estimate*, the *payment summary*, and *platform-specific elements* of the Google Ads Campaign Manager for YouTube:

- **Selecting a project goal & ad format:** The *selection of a project goal* and the *ad format* are so intertwined in video advertising via Google Ads that these two categories cannot be separated. The broad objectives that can be selected include "Video views," "Efficient reach," "Target Frequency," "Non-skippable reach," "Drive conversions," "Ad sequence," and "Audio." In this context, the term "Video views" refers to the number of views and engagement metrics from individuals who are more likely to consider the products or brand in question. The payment is only initiated when a user elects to view the advertisement.

Additionally, the advertisements can be classified as either skippable[12] or non-skippable,[13] including in-stream,[14] in-feed,[15] and Shorts[16] advertisements. The goal "Efficient reach" is employed to denote the most cost-effective means of reaching a target audience, utilizing a combination of bumper,[17] skippable in-stream, in-feed, and Shorts advertisements. The "Target Frequency" feature enables advertisers to reach the same audience multiple times with a variety of ad formats, including skippable in-stream ads, non-skippable in-stream ads, and bumper ads. The "Non-skippable reach" feature enables advertisers to reach their target audience with up to 15 seconds of non-skippable in-stream ads. The objective, "Drive conversions," is designed to facilitate a greater number of conversions through the use of video advertisements that are crafted to foster meaningful interactions. The "Ad sequence" functionality enables the presentation of a narrative through the sequential display of advertisements to individual viewers. This approach allows for the incorporation of both skippable and non-skippable in-stream advertisements, as well as bumper ads, within a single sequence. The project goal, "Audio," enables you to connect with your target audience while they are engaged with audio content on YouTube through the use of audio-based advertisements.

---

[12] These advertisements are designed to be skippable, typically after a period of 5 s or less. This feature enables users to circumvent the full advertisement if they so choose, allowing them to continue viewing their desired content without interruption.

[13] It is a requirement that the viewer watches the entirety of the advertisement before proceeding to the desired content. Typically, the advertisements are of a shorter duration, lasting approximately 15–20 s.

[14] Video advertisements are classified as either pre-roll, mid-roll, or post-roll, depending on their position in relation to the primary video content on platforms such as YouTube. They may be either skippable or non-skippable, and are designed to blend seamlessly into the surrounding content.

[15] The advertisements are displayed within a feed of content, such as a social media news feed or a list of videos. They are designed to blend in with other content and can include a thumbnail, title, and brief description, thereby encouraging users to click and watch.

[16] These are ads that appear specifically within YouTube Shorts, which is YouTube's platform for short, vertical videos. Similar to other ad types, Shorts ads can be skippable or non-skippable and are optimized for a brief and engaging experience on mobile devices.

[17] Bumper ads are a type of non-skippable advertisement that lasts up to 6 s. These brief ads are typically embedded before, during, or after a video and are designed to deliver a concise and memorable message. Due to their brevity and non-skippable nature, bumper ads are often employed to enhance brand awareness or reinforce a message in a condensed format. They are commonly observed on platforms such as YouTube.

- **Ad preview:** The *ad preview* appears within as soon as the video link has been added. In this view, an example of the display for mobile devices, computers, or TVs is possible. In this category, you can again choose between skippable in-stream display, in-feed video display, or bumper display. In addition, an explicit call to action[18] and a companion banner[19] can be set up.
- **Selection of target group and persona:** Since the data in Google Ads Manager is generated via user profiles (e.g., via the login status in Google Chrome), there are hardly any limits to the *selection of target group and persona* on YouTube. People can generally be segmented according to demographic criteria such as age, gender, parental status, or household income.[20] It is also possible to specify the location and language of potential customers in the default settings. In addition, it is also possible to define the context in which the video ad is to be delivered. In this context, a distinction is made between keywords, topics, and placements. Keywords are used to define the search queries made by users as a prerequisite for the placement of the video ad. For example, if a person searches for "cat videos" and one of the keywords predefined by the company is "cat," the video ad will probably be shown to this person in the future. Topics are much more general than keywords. One attempt is made to understand the search intention of the person searching and to play the video ad accordingly. For example, if someone searches for "diet tips," the topic "health" and the sub-topic "nutrition" are relevant. Depending on which category is selected, there are different numbers of sub-categories.
- **Duration:** The start date and end date of the campaign can be selected individually.
- **Daily budget:** The budget can be entered as a total budget for the campaign or as a *daily budget*. There are virtually no upper or lower

---

[18] A call to action (CTA) is a prompt in a marketing message that encourages the audience to take a specific action. This could be anything from "Click Here," "Buy Now," "Sign Up," "Subscribe," or "Learn More." The CTA is an essential element in advertisements, websites, emails, and other marketing materials, guiding the user toward the desired action and often serving as the next step in the sales or engagement process.

[19] Companion banners are image banners that are displayed next to the video ad. A user-defined image can be uploaded for the banner or an image can be generated from the channel banner.

[20] Targeting of household income is only available in selected country markets.

limits when entering the budget. In addition to the campaign or daily budget, a maximum CPV[21] bid can also be entered.
- **Result estimate:** The result estimate is given based on the campaign settings, but not based on budget or bid. As a result, campaign estimates are given in terms of possible ad impressions.
- **Payment summary:** The payment summary is based on the targeting, the campaign settings made, the campaign budget, and the bid for the respective conversion. The average budget expenditure is shown as an estimate for the cost-per-conversion.
- **Platform-specific elements:** When creating YouTube ad campaigns, there is a whole range of *platform-specific elements*. "Content to exclude" can be used to specify before, during, or after which content the ad should not be played. This setting is useful to prevent ads from being associated with certain websites, videos, channels, or apps that may not be suitable for your company. In contrast, the "Similar videos" function can be used to specify videos that are related or connected to the video ad. This function should be selected to ensure that the ad is delivered in connection with certain videos or content. The "Devices" setting can be used to select the devices (computer, smartphone, tablet, or TV) on which the ad is played. The "Frequency capping" setting can be used to limit how often ads in a campaign are shown to the same user. The "Advertising scheduler" allows you to select days and times of day when the ad should or should not be displayed.[22] By activating "Measurement by third-party providers," not only companies themselves, but also commissioned agencies or affiliated companies can access the campaign data. Finally, in the "Advertising networks" section, you can select whether the ad should be displayed in the YouTube search results and/or within YouTube videos and/or with video partners from the display network.

---

[21] Maximum CPV stands for the maximum cost-per-view and defines the maximum amount you are prepared to pay for a view of the ad.

[22] For example, in the consumer sector (B2C), the off-peak times and weekends are often well frequented, while in the B2B sector, the days Monday to Thursday between 8 a.m. and 4 p.m. and Friday from 8 a.m. to 12 p.m. are more popular.

Buyer personas are also crucial on YouTube to ensure that your video ads are served to the right people. YouTube offers multiple targeting options, but without a clear idea of who your ideal customers are, it will be difficult to create effective campaigns. Creating buyer personas for YouTube requires extensive research and data collection. Once you have defined your buyer personas, you can segment your audience on YouTube using targeting options. Keep in mind that creating video ads for YouTube in particular requires careful planning and creativity. As with any advertising campaign, it's crucial to monitor the performance of your YouTube ads and optimize them as needed. Again, pay attention to metrics such as reach, engagement rate, conversion rate, and click through rate. Modify either your ads, your buyer persona, or your budget to achieve improved results.

YouTube provides an excellent platform for placing video ads and reaching your target audience. By using buyer personas, you can ensure that your ads are served to the right people and that your message is delivered effectively. Make sure your video content is professional and engaging, and continuously optimize your personas and campaigns to get the best results.

3.4.4 TikTok

3.4.4.1 Characteristics of TikTok

TikTok is a social media platform that has become very popular in recent years. This platform offers users the opportunity to create and share short videos, usually set to music, in which they showcase their creativity, talent, and sense of humor. The platform is particularly popular with young people and has become a powerful tool for influencers, brands, and celebrities to connect with their audience. The origins of TikTok can be traced back to the Chinese app Douyin, which was released in 2016. Douyin quickly became popular in China. The following year, the company behind the app, ByteDance, launched a global version of the app called TikTok. The app quickly gained popularity around the world and was the most downloaded app on the App Store and Google Play in 2019. TikTok is a unique platform that combines elements of other popular social media platforms such as Instagram and YouTube. Users can create and upload short videos, which are usually between 15 and 60 seconds long and can be accompanied by music. Filters, effects, and other editing tools can also be used. Similar to most social media platforms, it is also possible to interact with other members. This primarily includes commenting on and liking videos and following other users to have their videos displayed in the newsfeed (Xu et al., 2019; Savic, 2021).

TikTok's algorithm is a complex system that determines which videos are shown to which members. The algorithm takes into account a variety of factors, such as user engagement with the video, the number of likes and comments, and the relevance of the video to the user's interests. The algorithm also takes into account the user's behavior in the app. This means that if a user frequently watches videos on a certain topic, the algorithm will show that person more videos on that topic. Videos that are engaging and are watched by users over a longer period of time are more likely to be shown to more users (Ionescu & Licu, 2023).

3.4.4.2 Campaign Settings on TikTok

In recent years, TikTok has become a powerful tool for companies and brands to stay in touch with their audience. The platform offers a variety of features that businesses can use to promote their products or services, and it also provides access to a large audience. One of the primary methods for businesses to leverage TikTok is through sponsored posts. These are videos created by companies and offered to users on the platform. These videos can be targeted to specific audiences based on demographics, interests, and behaviors (Alby et al., 2011). The following overview summarizes the areas of *selecting a project goal*, *ad format*, the *ad preview*, the *selection of target group and persona*, the *duration*, the *daily budget*, the *result estimate*, the *payment summary*, and *platform-specific elements* of the TikTok Ads Manager:

- **Selection of a project goal:** The *selection of a project goal* on TikTok is divided into main categories and subcategories. The main categories move along the customer journey, similar to other ad managers. These are "Awareness," "Consideration," and "Conversions." In the "Awareness" area, the "Reach" sub-category can be used to increase product or brand awareness by displaying the ad to the maximum number of people. The subcategories "Traffic," "Video views," and "Community interaction" can be found in the "Consideration" area. "Traffic" is used in particular to send more people to a destination on the company website or within the company app. "Video views" generate more views and interactions for the video ad. The sub-target "Community interaction" generates more page followers or profile visits. In the main category "Conversions," the subcategories "App promotion," "Lead generation," and "Website conversions" are available. The "App promotion" target project inspires more users to install and use the company app. The "lead generation" captures leads for the company and the "Website conversions" promote valuable actions on the company website.

- **Ad format:** On TikTok, ads are displayed as a single video, as a single image, or as collection ad. Collection ads generate a combination of instant experiences that can be used in the ad.
- **Ad preview:** The *ad preview is* located on the right-hand side and is displayed by using the optimization tool in a way that corresponds to the requirements of the respective placement.
- **Selection of target group and persona:** Comprehensive segmentation and targeting categories are available on TikTok. The four main categories in this context are "Demographics," "Audience," "Interests and Behaviors," and "Devices." In the "Demographics" category, the location, gender, age, spending power[23] and languages of the target group can be defined. In the "Audience" category, existing target groups can be included or excluded. The lookalike targeting[24] of

---

[23] TikTok's "Spending Power Targeting" feature enables advertisers to reach users with a high propensity to make significant purchases. By leveraging historical data, TikTok identifies users who have demonstrated purchasing behaviour aligned with the advertiser's goals. This feature is particularly beneficial for businesses offering premium products or services, as it helps in reaching those users most likely to convert, making ad campaigns more efficient and cost-effective.

[24] In lookalike targeting, a group of members of a social network that shares certain characteristics with another group of members is used for advertising purposes. For example, if you have run a very successful advertising campaign in the past, lookalike targeting offers the opportunity to

certain groups can also be defined as an inclusion or exclusion criterion. In the "Interests & Behavior" section, users' areas of interest and their behavior on the platform can be defined. The definition of interests is very diverse and can include interests such as "news & entertainment," "culture & art," "sports & leisure," "food and drink," "financial services," or "DIY." In the "Behavior" category, the three sub-categories "Video interactions," "Creator interactions," or "Hashtag interactions" can be defined. For "Video interactions," you can specify whether users have watched certain videos to the end or interacted with the content, what type of videos they have interacted with and whether the desired behavior has taken place within the past 7 or 15 days. The "Creator interactions" setting makes it possible to reach people who follow or have viewed the profiles of certain creators. "Hashtag interactions" offer the opportunity to reach users who have interacted more frequently with posts with certain hashtags in the past. In the "Device" section, certain operating system versions, device models, connection types, mobile providers, or device prices can be selected as targeting options.

- **Duration:** The *duration of* the advertising campaign can start from a specified start date or be executed within a date range. Here you can also specify whether the ad should be displayed throughout the day on all days of the week or only within a certain period and/or on certain days.
- **Daily budget:** The budget can be specified as a *daily* budget or as a total budget for the duration of the campaign.
- **Result estimate:** The *result estimate* is displayed on the right-hand side of the screen and changes depending on the campaign settings. The predicted results are displayed on TikTok as an estimate of the daily reach. Target groups with members under the age of 18 are excluded from the display of the expected daily reach. However, the delivery of the ad to users between the ages of 13 and 17 is not affected.
- **Payment summary:** The *payment summary* is determined by the daily or total budget and is therefore not explicitly presented.

"duplicate" this campaign without addressing exactly the same target group (Popov & Iakovleva, 2018).

- **Platform-specific elements:** As a relatively young and unique social media platform, TikTok has a whole range of platform-specific elements and setting options. For example, there is the option of A/B testing.[25] With A/B testing, the performance of two variants of an ad can be compared in the TikTok Ads Manager. Future campaigns can be improved in this way. In the Placement section, you can select whether the ad should only be displayed on TikTok or also via a global network of premium publishers. In addition, in this area you can set whether comments are permitted, whether video downloads should be enabled and whether the video can be shared. In the "Bids and optimization" section, the optimization target (e.g., click) and the bidding strategy can be adjusted. It is also possible to set an upper frequency limit. You can choose between the three placement options "Show ads no more than 3 times every 7 days," "Show ads more than once a day" and a "Custom frequency cap."

TikTok users are often young, trend-sensitive, and focused on entertaining content. Your buyer personas should reflect these characteristics and be enriched with components and data from the TikTok Ads Manager. TikTok offers various audience segmentation options to ensure that your ads reach the right users. Creating TikTok ads requires creativity and an understanding of the platform. To ensure the success of your TikTok ads, it is crucial to monitor performance and make continuous optimizations. Pay attention to metrics such as the reach, engagement rate, conversion rate, and click through rate of your ads. Experiment with different content and audience segmentation to get the best results.

TikTok offers an exciting platform for creative and entertaining ads, especially for brands looking to target a younger audience. By using buyer personas, you can ensure that your ads appeal to the needs and interests

---

[25] A/B testing is a method used in marketing and product development to evaluate the relative performance of two versions of a variable (such as a webpage, advertisement, or app feature). Version A is the control, and version B is the variation. Performance is typically measured in terms of user engagement, conversion rates, or other key metrics. On TikTok, this process is referred to as split testing. It serves the same purpose as other forms of A/B testing, allowing advertisers to optimise their campaigns by comparing different ad variations to determine which is most effective.

of your target audience. Stay flexible and continually adapt your strategy to respond to the evolving TikTok community and current trends.

3.5 Outlook

The world of social media is constantly evolving, with new platforms and trends popping up regularly. To keep your finger on the pulse and continuously optimize your online advertising, you should be open to new opportunities. Test new platforms that might appeal to your target audience and explore current trends such as live streaming, stories, or interactive content. Observe how these new approaches resonate with your target audience and adjust your strategy accordingly. This doesn't mean you have to jump on every new platform all the time, but it's important to stay curious and be willing to explore new ways to reach your target audience.

Applying the concept of buyer personas to the creation of online advertising on social media is a dynamic process that requires continuous adjustments. The combination of clearly defining your target audience, selecting the right platforms, using ad manager tools, and personalized content creation are the keys to success. Ongoing monitoring and optimization of your campaigns and a willingness to test new platforms and trends will ensure that you are always able to communicate effectively with your target audience and achieve your marketing goals. Buyer personas are a powerful tool to optimize your online advertising on social media and build long-term engagement with your target audience.

References

Alby, T., Dragan, A., Blahudka, R., Bottler, D., Buddenberg, D., Daul, C., et al. (2011). *Brand evolution: Modern brand management in the digital age.* Springer-Verlag.

Al-Maroof, R., Ayoubi, K., Alhumaid, K., Aburayya, A., Alshurideh, M., Alfaisal, R., & Salloum, S. (2021). The acceptance of social media video for knowledge acquisition, sharing and application: A comparative study among

YouYube users and TikTok users' for medical purposes. *International Journal of Data and Network Science, 5*(3), 197–214.

Appel, M., Marker, C., & Gnambs, T. (2020a). Are social media ruining our lives? A review of meta-analytic evidence. *Review of General Psychology, 24*(1), 60–74.

Appel, G., Grewal, L., Hadi, R., & Stephen, A. T. (2020b). The future of social media in marketing. *Journal of the Academy of Marketing Science, 48*(1), 79–95.

Arya, V., Paul, J., & Sethi, D. (2022). Like it or not! Brand communication on social networking sites triggers consumer-based brand equity. *International Journal of Consumer Studies, 46*(4), 1381–1398.

Auxier, B., & Anderson, M. (2021). Social media use in 2021. *Pew Research Center, 1*, 1–4.

Basit, A., Nurlukman, A. D., & Kosasih, A. (2020). The Effect of social media destination branding: The use of facebook and instagram. In *Tarumanagara international conference on the applications of social sciences and humanities (TICASH 2019)*. Atlantis Press.

Bekos, P., Papadopoulos, P., Markatos, E. P., & Kourtellis, N. (2022). The Hitchhiker's guide to Facebook web tracking with invisible pixels and click IDs. arXiv preprint arXiv:2208.00710.

Belanche, D., Flavián, C., & Pérez-Rueda, A. (2020). Brand recall of skippable vs non-skippable ads in YouTube: Readapting information and arousal to active audiences. *Online Information Review, 44*(3), 545–562.

Bernhardt, G. (2024). *Top 10 most popular social media platforms.* https://www.shopify.com/blog/most-popular-social-media-platforms. Accessed 19 Aug.

Boffone, T. (2022). Do you want to make a TikTok? Is it time to BeReal?: Gen Z, social media, and digital literacies. *Journal of Language & Literacy Education, 18*(2), 1–7.

Bouwman, H., de Reuver, M., & Nikou, S. (2017). *The impact of digitalization on business models: How IT artefacts, social media, and big data force firms to innovate their business model.* Springer Gabler.

Chawla, Y., & Chodak, G. (2021). Social media marketing for businesses: Organic promotions of web-links on Facebook. *Journal of Business Research, 135*, 49–65.

de Moraes, R. M., Sadjadpour, H. R., & Garcia-Luna-Aceves, J. J. (2007). Many-to-many communication: A new approach for collaboration in manets. In *IEEE INFOCOM 2007-26th IEEE international conference on computer communications*. IEEE.

Dehghani, M., Niaki, M. K., Ramezani, I., & Sali, R. (2016). Evaluating the influence of YouTube advertising for attraction of young customers. *Computers in Human Behavior, 59*, 165–172.

Endeley, R. E. (2017). End-to-end encryption in messaging services and national security – Case of WhatsApp messenger. *Journal of Information Security, 9*(1), 95–99.

Febriyantoro, M. T. (2020). Exploring YouTube marketing communication: Brand awareness, brand image and purchase intention in the millennial generation. *Cogent Business & Management, 7*(1), 1787733.

Fetissova, P. (2022). *Facebook conversion attribution 2023*. https://redtrack.io/blog/facebook-conversion-attribution-explained/. Accessed 09 May 2023.

Fink. (2021). *Drivers of user engagement in influencer branding : An empirical analysis of brand-related user-generated content on Instagram* (1st ed.). Springer Fachmedien.

Fuchs, C. (2021). *Social media: A critical introduction*. Sage.

Garrity, C. P. (2022). A/B testing in social media. In *The SAGE handbook of social media marketing*.

Gebel, A. (2020). *Social media in tourism marketing*. Springer Gabler.

Guetz, B., & Bidmon, S. (2022a). The impact of social influence on the intention to use physician rating websites: Moderated mediation analysis using a mixed methods approach. *Journal of Medical Internet Research, 24*(11), e37505.

Guetz, B., & Bidmon, S. (2022b). Awareness of and interaction with physician rating websites: A cross-sectional study in Austria. *PLoS One, 17*(12), e0278510.

Gummesson, E. (2004). From one-to-one to many-to-many marketing. In *Service excellence in management: Interdisciplinary contributions, proceedings from the QUIS 9 symposium*. Karlstad University.

Haidari, M., Katawazai, R., & Yusof, S. M. (2020). The use of social media and wikis in teaching writing skills: A review article.

Hoda, N., Ahmad, N., Alqahtani, H., & Naim, A. (2022). Social networking site usage, intensity and online social capital: A comparative study of LinkedIn and Facebook users with implications on technology-assisted learning. *International Journal of Emerging Technologies in Learning, 17*(9), 52–66.

Hofmann, M., & Mertiens, M. (2012). *Customer lifetime value management: Creating and increasing customer value: Concepts, strategies, practical examples*. Gabler.

Hu, Y., Shin, J., & Tang, Z. (2016). Incentive problems in performance-based online advertising pricing: Cost per click vs. cost per action. *Management Science, 62*(7), 2022–2038.

Huertas, A., & Marine-Roig, E. (2016). User reactions to destination brand contents in social media. *Information Technology & Tourism, 15*(4), 291–315.

Iannelli, L., Giglietto, F., Rossi, L., & Zurovac, E. (2020). Facebook digital traces for survey research: Assessing the efficiency and effectiveness of a Facebook Ad–based procedure for recruiting online survey respondents in niche and difficult-to-reach populations. *Social Science Computer Review, 38*(4), 462–476.

Ionescu, C. G., & Licu, M. (2023). Are TikTok algorithms influencing users' self-perceived identities and personal values? A mini review. *Social Sciences, 12*(8), 1–9.

Jacobson, J., Gruzd, A., & Hernández-García, Á. (2020). Social media marketing: Who is watching the watchers? *Journal of Retailing and Consumer Services, 53*, 101774.

Jadczak, M. (2023, September 8). Creating Facebook and Instagram analytics reports: A guide. *NapoleonCat*. https://napoleoncat.com/blog/facebook-and-instagram-reports/. Accessed 9 May 2023.

Jansasoy, J. & Jansasoy, J. (2023). *9 popular types of social media content to grow your brand*. https://sproutsocial.com/insights/types-of-social-media-content/. Accessed 9 Nove 2023.

Jensen, K. B. (2022). *Media convergence: The three degrees of network, mass, and interpersonal communication*. Routledge.

Linkedin (2022). LinkedIn Marketing Solutions. https://business.linkedin.com/de-de/marketing-solutions/. Accessed 10 Nov 2022.

Lipsman, A., Mudd, G., Rich, M., & Bruich, S. (2012). The power of "like": How brands reach (and influence) fans through social-media marketing. *Journal of Advertising Research, 52*(1), 40–52.

Liu, X., Min, Q., & Han, S. (2020). Understanding users' continuous content contribution behaviors on microblogs: An integrated perspective of uses and gratification theory and social influence theory. *Behavior & Information Technology, 39*(5), 525–543.

Macarthy, A. (2021). *500 social media marketing tips: Essential advice, hints and strategy for business: facebook, twitter, pinterest, Google+, YouTube, Instagram, LinkedIn, and more*. Easy Kindle E-Book.

Marshall, P., Meloche, T., & Regnerus, B. (2020). *Ultimate guide to Facebook advertising*. Entrepreneur Press.

Mezghani, M., On-At, S., Péninou, A., Canut, M. F., Zayani, C. A., Amous, I., & Sedes, F. (2015). A case study on the influence of the user profile enrichment on buzz propagation in social media: Experiments on delicious. In *East European conference on advances in databases and information systems*. Springer.

Moniz, N., & Torgo, L. (2018). Multi-source social feedback of online news feeds. arXiv preprint arXiv:1801.07055.

Moon, H., Lee, T., Seo, J., Park, C., Eo, S., Aiyanyo, I. D., et al. (2022). Return on advertising spend prediction with task decomposition-based LSTM model. *Mathematics, 10*(10), 1637.

Müller, J., & Christandl, F. (2019). Content is king – But who is the king of kings? The effect of content marketing, sponsored content & user-generated content on brand responses. *Computers in Human Behavior, 96*, 46–55.

Orzan, M. C., Zara, A. I., Căescu, Ş. C., Constantinescu, M. E., & Orzan, O. A. (2021). Social media networks as a business environment, during COVID-19 crisis. *Revista de Management Comparat International, 22*(1), 64–73.

Papadopoulos, S., Kompatsiaris, Y., Vakali, A., & Spyridonos, P. (2012). Community detection in social media. *Data Mining and Knowledge Discovery, 24*(3), 515–554.

Peng, J., Agarwal, A., Hosanagar, K., & Iyengar, R. (2018). Network overlap and content sharing on social media platforms. *Journal of Marketing Research, 55*(4), 571–585.

Petrosyan, A. (2024). *Number of internet and social media users worldwide as of July 2024*. https://www.statista.com/statistics/617136/digital-population-worldwide/#:~:text=Worldwide%20digital%20population%202024&text=As%20of%20April%202024%2C%20there,population%2C%20were%20social%20media%20users. Accessed 09 May 2023.

Pócs, D., Adamovits, O., Watti, J., Kovács, R., & Kelemen, O. (2021). Facebook users' interactions, organic reach, and engagement in a smoking cessation intervention: Content analysis. *Journal of Medical Internet Research, 23*(6), e27853.

Popov, A., & Iakovleva, D. (2018). Adaptive look-alike targeting in social networks advertising. *Procedia Computer Science, 136*, 255–264.

Radcliffe, D. (2021). Audio chatrooms like Clubhouse have become the hot new media by tapping into the age-old appeal of the human voice. *The Conversation*.

Reddy, S. G., Sadhu, A. K. R., Muravev, M., Brazhenko, D., & Parfenov, M. (2023). Harnessing the power of generative artificial intelligence for dynamic content personalization in customer relationship management systems: A data-driven framework for optimizing customer engagement and experience. *Journal of AI-Assisted Scientific Discovery, 3*(2), 379–395.

Savic, M. (2021). Research perspectives on TikTok & its Legacy Appsl from musical. Ly to TikTok: Social construction of 2020's Most downloaded short-video app. *International Journal of Communication, 15*, 22.

Sheng, J. T., & Kairam, S. R. (2020). From virtual strangers to irl friends: Relationship development in livestreaming communities on twitch. *Proceedings of the ACM on Human-Computer Interaction, 4*(CSCW2), 1–34.

Shepherd, J. (2024). *41 essential LinkedIn statistics you need to know in 2024.* https://thesocialshepherd.com/blog/linkedin-statistics Accessed 19 Aug 2024.

Tafesse, W., & Wien, A. (2017). A framework for categorizing social media posts. *Cogent Business & Management, 4*(1), 1284390.

Vangelov, N. (2019). Efficient communication through influencer marketing. *Styles of Communication, 11*(1).

Wehrli, S., Irrgang, C., Scott, M., Arnrich, B., & Boender, T. S. (2024). The role of the (in) accessibility of social media data for infodemic management: A public health perspective on the situation in the European Union in march 2024. *Frontiers in Public Health, 12*, 1378412.

Wong, L. (2022). *How to write your best social media bio.* https://blog.hootsuite.com/social-media-bio/. Accessed 19 Aug 2024.

Wong, R. Y., & Nguyen, T. (2021). Timelines: A world-building activity for values advocacy. In *Proceedings of the 2021 CHI conference on human factors in computing systems* (pp. 1–15).

Xu, L., Yan, X., & Zhang, Z. (2019). Research on the causes of the "TikTok" app becoming popular and the existing problems. *Journal of Advanced Management Science, 7*(2).

Yang, Y., & Zhai, P. (2022). Click-through rate prediction in online advertising: A literature review. *Information Processing & Management, 59*(2), 102853.

Zhu, B. (2021). Clubhouse: A popular audio social application. In *2021 international conference on public relations and social sciences (ICPRSS 2021)*. Atlantis Press.

4

Search Engine Advertising

What You Will Take Away from This Chapter

- You will get an understanding of how companies can leverage search engines for advertising purposes.
- You will understand the effective use of buyer personas for search engine advertising.
- You will become aware of the metrics used to measure the success of search engine advertising.
- You will know the most utilized search engines for advertising purposes and how to utilize buyer personas on them.

4.1 SEA in a Nutshell

Search engine advertising is a digital marketing strategy that involves bidding on specific keywords or key terms in order to have ads displayed at the top of search engine results pages. These ads are displayed above the organic search results.[1] This type of advertising is becoming increasingly popular as more and more consumers use search engines to find products and services (Yang et al., 2016).

The use of search engine advertising offers several advantages, including (Nyagadza, 2022):

- *Increased visibility*: Search engine advertising can help businesses increase their visibility, making it more likely that potential customers will find and click on their ads.
- *Targeted advertising*: With search engine advertising, companies can place targeted advertising for specific keywords and terms and thus reach consumers who are actively searching for the products or services offered.
- *Measurable results*: Search engine advertising platforms provide companies with detailed metrics and analytics that make it easier for them to track the performance of their campaigns and make adjustments as needed.
- *Cost efficiency*: In contrast to conventional forms of advertising, companies can set a budget for search engine advertising and only pay when someone clicks on their ad or makes a conversion.[2] This makes search engine advertising a cost-efficient way to reach potential customers.

In summary, search engine advertising is a cost-effective and highly targeted form of digital marketing that companies can use to increase their visibility and reach potential customers. With the right approach, companies of all sizes can use search engine advertising to achieve their

---

[1] Organic search results are listings on a search engine results page (SERP) that appear naturally based on their relevance to the search query. Unlike paid advertisements, organic search results are not influenced by external factors and are instead ranked by the search engine's algorithms based on factors like keyword relevance, website authority, and user engagement. Organic search results are distinct from paid search results, which are ads that appear at the top or bottom of a SERP and are marked as sponsored or ads.

[2] In the field of search engine advertising, a conversion is a measurable activity that is carried out by (potential) customers. This includes, for example, clicking on the telephone number and the associated telephone call or filling out and sending a form.

marketing goals. Search engine ads—especially the industry leader Google Ads—can be used to create a variety of different advertising formats. The most famous ad type in this context is the *search ad*, but there are also other formats such as *display ads, shopping ads, video,* or *app ads*. The following overview summarizes the most common ad formats that can be displayed via search engines:

- **Search ads**: *Search ads* are paid advertisements that are placed above or below organic search engine results. These ads can be used to promote websites, products, or services and are usually billed via a pay-per-click or pay-per-conversion model, where the advertiser pays each time a person clicks on one of the ads placed or performs a certain action. Companies specify keywords for which they want their ads to appear and bid on the cost they are willing to pay per click or per conversion. The search engine then uses an auction-based system to determine which ads should appear in response to a person's search query. The ads are ranked based on factors such as bid amount, relevance, and quality score of the ad and the landing page. One of the main benefits of search ads is that they allow companies to reach a highly targeted audience. Since users are actively searching for a specific product or service, search ads are more likely to be seen by people who are already interested in what the company has to offer. In addition, search ads offer measurable results as companies can track how many clicks and conversions their ads generate (Levy, 2021; Halavais, 2017).
- **Display ads**: Display ads are an advertising tool for marketing products, services, or brands. This type of ad is usually placed on websites. Display ads are designed to attract the viewer's attention and persuade them to take a specific action, e.g., to visit a website, make a purchase, or sign up for a newsletter. There are different types of display ads, including banner ads, which convey a static advertising message, animated ads, which superimpose a static and a moving image, or video ads. Display advertising offers several advantages, including (Katz, 2016):

- *Reach*: Display ads can reach a large audience, especially if they are placed on popular websites.
- *Audience targeting*: Display ads can be targeted to specific audiences based on factors such as location, age, gender, interests, and browsing behavior.
- *Brand awareness:* Display ads can help to increase brand awareness and recognition among target groups.
- *Measurable results:* Display advertising campaigns can be measured and optimized using key figures such as impressions, clicks, conversions, and return on investment (ROI).

In summary, display ads can be an effective advertising medium for promoting products, services, and brands online. By targeting specific audiences and presenting clear added value, display ads can help to increase brand awareness and drive conversions (Bala & Verma, 2018).

- **Shopping ads**: Shopping ads are an advertising format that can be used to promote companies, brands, products, and services online. They are an extremely effective way for companies to reach potential customers and increase sales, as they provide users with a clear and visually appealing presentation of the offer. Shopping ads are often displayed at the top of the search engine results list and are characterized by the immediate display of product image and price. To maximize the effectiveness of Shopping ads, companies need to regularly monitor and adjust their campaigns. This can include making changes to bids, adjusting targeting criteria, and updating the product data feed. An important factor in optimizing the performance of Shopping ads is relevance. Ads that are highly relevant to users are more likely to be clicked on, which can lead to higher conversion rates. Companies should therefore focus on targeting their ads to the users who are most likely to be interested in their products or services (Bayer et al., 2020).
- **Video ads**: Video ads are an advertising format that uses video content to promote companies, brands, products, and services. They are a highly engaging form of advertising that can capture users' attention and effectively convey important messages. There are different types

of video ads, including in-stream ads, which play before, during, or after a video on a platform, or outstream ads, which are displayed outside of video content on websites and social media platforms. To maximize the effectiveness of video ads, companies need to regularly monitor and adjust their campaigns. This can include changes to targeting criteria, updating video content, and adjusting budgets. An important factor in optimizing video ad performance is again relevance. Ads that are highly relevant to users are more likely to be viewed to the end, which can lead to higher conversion rates. Companies should therefore focus on targeting their video ads to the users who are most likely to be interested in their products or services (Belanche et al., 2017).

- **App ads:** The number of mobile apps has increased significantly in recent years. Billions of people use smartphones and tablets to communicate, play games, shop, and stay connected. With so many people using apps, app ads have become a lucrative advertising medium, providing companies with a platform to promote their products and services to a large group of individuals. App ads are crucial not only for app developers, but for almost all businesses, as they can help reach a wider audience, increase visibility, and grow the customer base. They also provide a way for businesses to monetize their apps and generate revenue from their investments in development and marketing. There are different types of app ads, including banner ads, video ads, or native ads. Each type of app ad has its own advantages and disadvantages and the decision of which type to use depends on the target audience, goals, and budget. Planning a successful app ad requires careful consideration of several key factors, including target audience, budget, and advertising platform. It also requires setting clear goals and success metrics, choosing the right ad format and placement, and continuously testing and optimizing the campaign to achieve maximum results. Despite their potential benefits, app ads also come with some challenges. These include ad fraud, low engagement, and low conversion rates. Overcoming these challenges requires a combination of technical solutions, such as the use of ad fraud detection tools, creative solutions, such as the use of visually appealing ads, and a comprehensive understanding of target audiences. Nevertheless, the future of app ads looks bright as technology continues to evolve and new advertising platforms emerge. With the advent of machine learning and artificial intelligence, app ads are likely to become even more targeted, efficient, and effective, helping businesses reach the right people with the right message at the right time (Maddodi & Upadhyaya, 2024).

4.2 Basic Procedure

Search engine advertising is based on a pay-per-click or pay-per-conversion model, which means that companies only pay when someone clicks on their ad or performs a certain predefined conversion. To get started with search engine advertising, companies must first set up an account with a search advertising platform such as Google Ads or Microsoft Advertising. They then create and manage their ads via the platform, select terms for which their ads should appear and set a budget for the campaign (Jafarzadeh et al., 2015). Based on this, the target audience can be narrowed down using various criteria and the ad campaign can be created. The performance of the campaign can be tracked in real time and the campaign can be adapted if necessary. The following listicle provides an overview of the most common components of search engine advertising:

- **Selecting a project goal:** The *project goal*, which affects both the individual campaigns and the company goal, is an important principle of search engine marketing. Many search engine advertising providers offer a separate section for entering the *project goal* so that it can be applied to the corresponding campaign.
- **Campaign type:** There are various *campaign types* to choose from within search engine advertising. The "classic" campaign in this area is the search ad, which appears as soon as the relevant keywords are entered within an index-based search engine. Nevertheless, there are many other *campaign types* available in the search engine advertising environment, such as the aforementioned display ads, shopping ads, video ads, or app ads.

- **Ad preview**: Most ad managers offer an *ad preview* that allows users to check their own ads before they are published.
- **Keywords**: *Keywords* serve as the foundation for the majority of search ads. When creating the campaign terms are defined that users must enter in order for the campaign to be displayed. Some ad managers also offer the option of defining keyword options. The aim in this context is to define how precisely (or imprecisely) the selected search terms must be entered for the ad to appear.
- **Selection of target group and persona**: Similar to social media, the *selection of target group and persona* is also very diverse in the area of search engine advertising. The gender and age group can be specified, as can the hobbies, preferences, and behavioral patterns of the persona.
- **Duration**: Search engine campaigns can usually be limited in time. In most cases, however, it is also possible to run the campaign permanently and intervene on the platform to stop or adapt it if necessary.
- **Daily budget**: The *daily budget* indicates the amount of money that is available each day for the distribution of the campaign. The *daily budget* can usually be exceeded or fall short of by a certain amount. Over a longer campaign period, however, these budget peaks usually balance each other out.
- **Result estimate**: The *result estimate* provides a rough forecast of the reach and interactions that can be achieved with the publication of the campaign.
- **Payment summary:** Within the *payment summary*, the totals of the campaign costs are shown. These are often forecast on the basis of the estimated results.
- **Platform-specific elements**: Ad managers for search engines also have different platform-specific elements, depending on their origin, company affiliations, and orientation.

A thorough understanding of your target group is necessary for the successful development of search engine advertising. Buyer personas are therefore crucial in search engine marketing. The second chapter provides a detailed guide to creating buyer personas in general. However, there is a set process that should be followed in order to use them efficiently in search engine advertising. Nevertheless, it is important to note that the process for using buyer personas in search engine marketing can vary depending on the company, industry, and target market. Each company has specific requirements and challenges that require customization. However, a good process flow can serve as a general reference. In the following section, we will outline the usual process that can be used as a guideline for creating customized search engine advertising using buyer personas. However, this process can be modified and extended to meet the individual needs of your business.

Step 1: The Definition of Buyer Personas
Before creating your search engine advertising, it is necessary to develop or refine your buyer personas. This step involves researching and analyzing your target audience to gain a better understanding of their needs, challenges, behaviors, and preferences. You can use customer surveys, data analysis, and other market research methods to gather reliable information. These insights allow you to create detailed buyer personas that represent different segments of your target group.

Step 2: Selecting the Right Search Engines
Choosing the right search engines for advertising with buyer personas requires careful consideration. In many regions, Google is undoubtedly the dominant search engine and will therefore be indispensable for reaching the broadest target groups. However, it is important to note that for certain personas, other search engines such as Bing or Yandex could also play a role. Although these search engines have a smaller market share, they attract specific user groups that may be of interest to certain companies and products. Therefore, when choosing search engines, it is advisable to consider not only the global market leader but also regional or niche search engines to ensure that your advertising campaigns reach the relevant target groups effectively.

Step 3: Enrichment of the Buyer Persona with Data from the Search Engine Advertising Platforms
Enriching the buyer persona with data from search engine advertising platforms is a valuable step toward optimizing your online advertising campaigns and better understanding your target group. Integrate

demographic criteria as well as the target group segments of the respective advertising platform even more into your existing persona(s). In the longer term, by integrating behavioral data, you can create tailored and relevant ads that appeal to your potential customers and lead to better results. This ongoing process allows you to continuously improve your advertising strategy and adapt to the changing needs of your target audience.

Step 4: Creating Ads for Search Engine Advertising with Buyer Personas

Ad creation for search advertising with buyer personas is a critical step in ensuring that your advertising campaigns are successful. If you have carefully developed your buyer personas and enriched them with data from the search engine advertising platforms, you are well equipped to create relevant and engaging ads. Use the insights gained to select the right keywords, craft the messages and offers that appeal to your target audience, and the ad formats that best suit their preferences. Using buyer personas in ad creation allows you to better target your campaigns and ensure that you are accurately addressing the needs and interests of your potential customers. This helps to increase the efficiency of your search engine advertising and achieve better results.

Step 5: Continuous Monitoring and Optimization

Once you have tailored your ads to the needs and interests of your target group, you should regularly monitor the performance of your ads. This means keeping an eye on metrics such as clicks, impressions, click through rate, and cost per click. This data provides valuable insights to adjust ads, optimize keywords, and manage budgets efficiently.[3] Your buyer personas serve as a guide for fine-tuning your campaigns as they provide a deeper understanding of your target audience's behaviors and preferences. This way, you can continuously optimize your search ads and ensure that they are effectively tailored to the needs of your potential customers.

---

[3] See Sect. 4.3

Creating online advertising with buyer personas in search engine advertising allows you to use personalization in your marketing strategy. By catering to the specific needs and interests of your target audience, you increase the relevance of your ads and maximize your chances of success. Although this process is time-consuming and requires continuous research and adjustments, the investment in personalized online advertising will be rewarded in the long run as it strengthens customer loyalty and promotes the growth of your business.

4.3 Measuring Success in the Area of Search Engine Advertising

Search engine advertising (SEA) is one of the most effective ways to create online visibility and reach potential customers. However, to maximize the success of SEA campaigns, the right metrics and analytics must be used. Basic SEA metrics include *clicks, impressions, click through rate,* and *cost per click. Clicks* symbolize the number of users who have clicked on an ad and serve as a significant indication of the ad's relevance. *Impressions* represent how often the ads were displayed on the search results pages. They show how often your ads were shown to potential customers. The *click through rate* is the ratio between the number of clicks on an ad and the number of ad impressions. It shows how effective ads are in search engines like Google by showing how many people click on the ad after seeing it. A high *click through rate* often indicates relevant and engaging ads. The *cost per click* represents the amount companies spend per individual click on their ads which is essential for budget management (Kleindienst, 2017).

In addition to the key figures and metrics mentioned above, *conversion tracking* and *return on investment (ROI)* are also essential for measuring the success of search engine campaigns. *Conversion tracking* can be used to determine how many users perform a desired action on the target website after clicking on the ad. These actions can be defined, for example, as filling out a contact form, purchasing a product, or downloading a brochure. In contrast to *conversion tracking, ROI* is one of the most important metrics in monetary performance measurement. It makes it possible to determine how effective search engine campaigns are in relation to the investments made. The *ROI* is determined by subtracting the costs from the revenue generated by *conversions*. In the second and final step, this result is divided by the costs (Li et al., 2016).

A/B tests also play an important role in the field of search engine advertising. These tests allow advertisers to create different versions of their ads and landing pages and deliver them to a randomly selected sample of their target group. By comparing key figures and metrics such as *click through rate, conversion rate,* and *return on investment,* they can gather objective data on which version performs best. A/B testing is an indispensable tool for optimizing ads, using budgets more efficiently, and ensuring that advertising messages are delivered effectively to the target audience (Pitikaris, 2023). In this context, the importance of attribution models must also be addressed. Attribution models are crucial to understanding the contribution of each interaction (be it a click or an impression) on the path to conversion. They offer different approaches, such as the first-touch[4] or last-touch[5] attribution model, to determine which interactions have the biggest impact on conversion. These models are essential to evaluate the effectiveness of your search engine advertising and make informed decisions to optimize the marketing strategy (Mehta & Singhal, 2020).

Evaluating search engine advertising performance plays a key role in ensuring the effectiveness of SEA campaigns and achieving your business goals. Selecting and monitoring appropriate metrics, implementing *conversion tracking,* optimizing ads, and ongoing analysis can ensure that the highest possible *return on investment is* achieved.

---

[4] The first-touch attribution model attributes the entire value of a conversion to the first interaction a user has on the path to conversion. It identifies and emphasizes the first contact with an ad or marketing channel as the main factor for conversion contribution (Restori, 2018).

[5] The last-touch attribution model attributes the entire value of a conversion to the last interaction a user had before completing the conversion. It focuses exclusively on the immediate preceding interaction and considers it to be the decisive factor for the conversion contribution (Mischke, 2023).

4.4 Application on Selected Search Engines

In the past 20 years, the advertising revenue of the industry giant Google has risen from 410 million US dollars in 2002 to over 224 billion US dollars in 2022 (Bianchi, 2023). Above all, this shows the enormous potential that search engines offer for advertisers. The following chapters provide examples of the online advertising process with buyer personas for the two largest search engines on the desktop search engine market.

4.4.1 Google

4.4.1.1 Characteristics of Google

As a search engine, Google has completely changed the way people search for information online. With more than 8.5 billion search queries per day, Google, which was founded in 1998 by Larry Page and Sergey Brin, has become the world's most popular search engine. The fast and precise search results, the clear user interface, and the cutting-edge technologies developed are among the factors responsible for the industry giant's success. In the first few years of its existence, Google experienced explosive growth and a series of innovations. AdWords,[6] a service that allows businesses to place ads on Google's search results pages, was developed by the company in 2000. The company's revenue from AdWords increased immediately, and it remains one of the company's top-selling products today (Shewale, 2024).

One of Google's most important innovations was the page rank algorithm, which evaluates the quantity and quality of links to a website in order to assess its importance. This enabled Google to deliver more accurate search results than its competitors, which helped the company to take the lead in the search engine market (Langville & Meyer, 2006).

Over the years, Google has continued to innovate and expand its offering. Gmail, a free email service launched in 2004, was particularly notable for its large storage space and sophisticated features. In 2005, the

---

[6] Today, Google Ads.

company bought the map company Keyhole, which served as the basis for Google Maps, a powerful tool for discovering and navigating between places. The ambition to digitize all the world's books is undoubtedly Google's most ambitious project to date. With the intention of building a huge online library accessible to everyone, the company began scanning millions of books from major libraries around the world in 2004. The initiative has sparked controversy due to copyright concerns, but has also been praised as a significant step forward in the democratization of knowledge (Chen et al., 2019, Mehta et al., 2019; Samuelson, 2009).

Google is and remains one of the most influential companies in the world. Its search engine is the main gateway to the Internet for billions of people and its services and technologies have transformed numerous industries. As Google continues to innovate and expand, the company is likely to continue to play an important role in the world of search engines for years to come (Desai & Vidyapeeth, 2019).

4.4.1.2 Campaign Settings on Google Ads

Google Ads is one of the most effective advertising platforms on the Internet and offers companies of all sizes the opportunity to place ads in Google's search results and on websites that use Google as an advertising partner. The goal of Google Ads is to help businesses reach more potential customers and strengthen their online presence. To create a Google Ads campaign, a Google Ads account must first be set up. Then a new campaign can be created by selecting the target group, budget, and ad type. The function of the Google Ads Manager when creating a search engine advertising campaign is described below. The areas of *selecting the project goal, ad format, ad preview, selection of target group and persona, duration, daily budget, results estimate, payment summary,* and *platform-specific elements* of the Google Ads Manager are summarized below:

- **Selecting a project goal:** The *project goal* within Google Ads Manager include "Sales," "Leads," "Website traffic," "App promotion," "Awareness and consideration," "Local store visits and promotions," or "Create a campaign without a goal's guidance." The "Sales" campaign objective is used to boost sales online, in apps, on the phone or in-store. The "Leads" campaign objective prompts users to take action. This action can be filling out and submitting a contact form or calling the retailer. "Website traffic" leads to more users visiting the company website. "App advertising" makes it possible to achieve more app installations and pre-registrations. If "awareness and consideration" is selected as the objective, display and/or video advertising is used to increase awareness of the company and the brand. The campaign objective "Local store visits and promotions" increases the number of visits to local stores or restaurants. Finally, the campaign objective "Create a campaign without a goal's guidance" offers the possibility to freely design the entire campaign. Search ads can only be developed within the campaign objectives "Sales," "Leads," "Website traffic," and "Create a campaign without a goal's guidance."

- **Ad format:** In general, Google Ads can be used to create "search campaigns," "campaigns for maximum performance," "display campaigns," "shopping campaigns," "video campaigns," "app campaigns, and "demand generation campaigns." "Search campaigns" are used to draw the attention of users with a high purchase intent to the product or company at the right time in Google searches. The "campaign for maximum performance" uses all Google channels to reach the target group. "Display campaigns" use more than 3 million apps and websites to reach potential customers. "Shopping campaigns" are used to present products to potential buyers during their research. "Video ads" appeal to users via YouTube and "app campaigns" increase the interaction figures for the app. Finally, "demand generation campaigns" assist in identifying and converting consumers through the use of immersive, relevant, and visual creatives that capture attention and prompt action at opportune moments. By integrating your best-performing video and image assets across entertainment-focused touchpoints, including YouTube, YouTube Shorts, Discover, and Gmail, Demand Gen enables you to reach over 3 billion monthly users as they stream, scroll, and connect.
- **Ad preview:** The advertisement is displayed in preview mode within the campaign manager. You can select the version intended for mobile devices, computers, or stationary devices.

- **Selection of target group and persona**: The campaign settings regarding the *selection of target group and persona* are divided into the areas "Locations," "Languages," "Audience segments," and "Keywords." In the "Locations" area, you can select where the target group is currently or frequently located or which regional area the target group is interested in. All countries and regions are selected as the default location for the campaign. However, it is also possible to restrict the campaign to individual countries (e.g., France), specific regions (e.g., Provence-Alpes-Côte d'Azur), or cities (e.g., Marseille). The "Languages" category determines which language the people to whom the ad is to be displayed should speak. The user's preferred language is derived from the browser language. The most extensive area in the *Selection of target group and persona* category is "Audience segments." In this area, you can search for target group characteristics. In addition, it is also possible to select specific characteristics within numerous predefined subcategories. The core category in the selection of target group and persona for search engine advertising is the selection of "Keywords." Keywords are key terms that potential customers use to search for products or services. If the keyword entered by the user via search mask of the search engine matches the selected keyword in the campaign manager, the probability that the search campaign will be displayed to the respective user increases.
- **Duration**: The advertising campaign can either be started from a predefined start date or within a specific time period. It is also possible to specify whether the ad should appear throughout the day on all days of the week or only during certain periods and/or on selected days.
- **Daily budget:** The budget can be defined as an average *daily budget* for the campaign.
- **Estimated results:** The estimated performance is visible for the first time after the keywords have been entered and changes according to the subsequent adjustments. This area shows the estimated conversions per week, the average costs per conversion, and the total weekly costs. Conversions can be increased accordingly by adjusting the budget. In addition, it is also possible to optimize the expected performance of the ad by entering additional keywords, improving the ad

title and text lines, adding additional information, and adding sitelinks.[7]
- **Payment summary:** The payment summary is determined by the daily budget which is presented as weekly costs in the results estimation area.
- **Platform-specific elements:** Google Ads is the Google Group's advertising tool. For this reason, this advertising manager can be used to design not only search ads, but also video ads, display ads, and other advertising formats. Accordingly, Google Ads has a whole range of platform-specific elements. A special feature of the platform in the area of search ads is, for example, that not only keywords can be selected that lead to the ad, but also a list of "keywords to be excluded"[8] can be created.

Buyer personas are crucial on Google Ads to ensure that your ads are shown to the right people. Without clearly defined buyer personas, it is almost impossible to select the appropriate keywords, ad copy, and audience segments. Google Ads offers an effective way to promote your business online and target your audience. By using buyer personas, you can ensure that your ads are tailored to the needs and interests of your customers. Monitor your campaigns regularly, optimize them continuously, and adjust your strategy to achieve the best results. With the right buyer personas and a well-thought-out Google Ads strategy, you can unleash the potential for great advertising success.

---

[7] Sitelinks are additional links that can be displayed in the search results of a search engine below the main website URL. They offer users a quicker way to access certain subpages or important areas of the website directly from the search results. These links are usually focused on the most relevant content on the website and are intended to improve user-friendliness and navigation options (Kelsey & Kelsey, 2017).

[8] Negative keywords are terms or phrases that you specify to ensure that your ads do not appear for certain search queries. Adding negative keywords is important to ensure that your ads only appear for relevant search queries and avoid unnecessary clicks and costs (Tavşanoğlu, 2018).

4.4.2 Bing

4.4.2.1 Characteristics of Bing

Bing was introduced as a search engine by Microsoft in 2009 (Ehrlich, 2009) and is now one of the most widely used search engines in the world. Although Bing does not enjoy the same market share as Google, it still has a significant presence and is used by millions of people worldwide. Bing was developed to enhance Microsoft's search engine offering and better integrate with its broad portfolio of products and services. The search engine was originally known as *Live Search*, but was later renamed Bing. Microsoft invested significant resources in the development of Bing to secure a place in the highly competitive search engine industry (Almukhtar et al., 2021).

Bing offers a wide range of functions that make it an attractive alternative to other search engines. These include *Microsoft Rewards*, *Rich Answers*, *Visual Search*, and integration with Windows and Microsoft products. *Microsoft Rewards* is a rewards program where users can earn points by using Bing for their search queries. These points can be redeemed for various rewards, including vouchers and gift cards. In addition, Bing offers *Rich Answers*, where it displays information on frequently searched terms directly on the search results page. These can be weather reports, conversion tables, sports results, and more. *Visual Search* allows users to search for images or parts of images to find similar results. This is especially useful when users are searching for products or places, they can visually recognize (Islam, 2023). Finally, Bing is deeply integrated into the Windows operating system and other Microsoft products. This includes, for example, Cortana voice search[9] and Bing Maps[10].

---

[9] Cortana voice search is a voice-controlled search function that was developed by Microsoft and is part of the Microsoft Windows operating system. Cortana enables users to direct search queries and commands to their computer or mobile device using their voice (Hong et al., 2021).
[10] Bing Maps is a web-based map service and geographic information system. It offers extensive map and geodata as well as a variety of functions that allow users to view maps, search for places, plan routes, and much more. Similar to other map services, Bing Maps offers various options for map use and location information (Ciepłuch et al., 2010).

4.4.2.2 Campaign Settings on Microsoft Advertising

In addition to the aforementioned advantages of the search engine, Bing offers a valuable platform for advertisers to present their products and services to a broad target group. While Bing may not have the same market share as Google in the search engine industry, it is still the second most used search engine in the desktop search engine market, according to the latest global rankings. Bing receives millions of searches per day and reaches a demographically diverse audience. As many advertisers are focused on Google Ads, there is often less competition on Bing. This can lead to lower cost per click and better visibility. In addition, Bing is integrated with the Windows operating system and other Microsoft products, which means that Bing ads can appear on multiple platforms, including PCs, tablets, and Xbox consoles. Advertising on Bing and connected platforms and company sites is done through the Microsoft Advertising Platform. This platform is similar to other online advertising platforms and offers a variety of advertising options such as search ads, display ads, video ads, shopping ads, or app ads (Brent, 2024).

Advertising with Microsoft Advertising offers a valuable complement to other advertising platforms. With less competition, precise targeting, and integration with Microsoft products, Bing Ads can be an effective way to promote your business and strengthen your online presence. By applying best practices and carefully optimizing your campaigns, you can realize the full potential of Bing Advertising. The following is an overview of how Microsoft Advertising works when creating a search engine advertising campaign. It summarizes the areas of *project goal selection*, *ad format*, *ad preview*, *target group and persona selection*, *duration*, *daily budget*, *results estimation*, *payment summary*, and *platform-specific elements* of the Microsoft Advertising Campaign Manager:

- **Selecting a project goal:** Microsoft Advertising offers a wide range of options to achieve specific campaign goals. These include "visits to my website," "visits to my business locations," "sales on my website," "phone calls for my company," "app installations," "selling products with Microsoft Shopping campaigns," "Microsoft Store ads," "video

views," and "ad views." The goal "visits to my website" is designed to drive more users to the target website, thereby increasing brand awareness and potentially generating leads. The project goal "visits to my business locations" aims to direct more people to physical locations such as stores, offices, or events. "Sales on my website" focuses on encouraging specific actions on the website, such as making a purchase or filling out a form. The goal "phone calls for my company" generates new phone calls to at least one of the company's phone numbers by prominently displaying the number in ads. If "app installations" is selected as the project goal, it increases the number of installations of the company's mobile app. The goal "selling products with Microsoft Shopping campaigns" promotes products through Microsoft Shopping ads, akin to showcasing items in a physical catalog. "Microsoft Store ads" are used to advertise applications and games in the Microsoft Store. The goal "video views" is intended to increase the views of video ads and convey the brand message. Finally, "ad views" lead to ads being displayed more frequently in Microsoft Advertising, thus enhancing the visibility and awareness of the brand.
- **Ad format:** Microsoft Advertising allows the creation of various types of ads, including "search ads," "display ads," "video ads," "shopping ads," and "app ads." "Search ads" are targeted at users who are actively searching for specific products or services, and they appear alongside search engine results. "Display ads" involve visual advertisements that are shown across websites and apps, enhancing brand visibility. "Video ads" engage users through multimedia content on platforms such as Microsoft Edge or Outlook. "Shopping ads" showcase products directly in search results, making it easier for users to find and purchase items. Finally, "app ads" are designed to promote mobile app installations by advertising directly in relevant search results or across the Microsoft network.
- **Ad preview:** The ad is displayed in preview mode in the Campaign Manager, where you can choose between the preview for mobile devices and that for computers or stationary devices.
- **Selection of target group and persona:** In Microsoft Advertising, the *selection of target group and persona* starts with determining the "Location" and "Language" of the audience that should see the ad. In

the "Location" section, advertisers can choose whether the ad should be shown in all available countries and regions or only in specific locations. Additionally, there is an option to target people based on whether they are physically in the selected locations or if they have shown interest in or searched for information about these locations. In the "Language" section, advertisers can specify the language that the audience should speak, which is typically derived from the user's browser language settings. Further segmentation can be done in the "Target group" area, where there are different target groups available. These groups can be defined by various interests, such as people interested in "music clubs," "education/foreign programs," or "dog food and accessories."

- **Duration:** The *duration of* the campaign can be entered within the advanced campaign settings including a start and an end date. It is also possible to publish the campaign on certain days at certain start and end times with bid adjustment. The publication period can be set to 12 h or 24 h and the desired time zone can be adjusted accordingly.
- **Daily budget:** The *daily budget* in Microsoft Advertising is specified at the beginning of the campaign setup as the average amount to be spent each day in the currency of your choice. During this step, you can choose between different bidding strategies, including "Enhanced CPC" and "Maximize clicks." If the "Enhanced CPC" bidding strategy is selected, the bid is automatically adjusted to optimize for conversions, with the aim of getting more conversions while staying within the budget. On the other hand, with the "Maximize clicks" strategy, the bid is set to achieve as many clicks as possible on the ads within the daily budget.
- **Result estimate:** The *result estimate* is based on estimated monthly clicks, estimated monthly impressions and estimated monthly costs. This estimate changes depending on the daily budget and bidding strategy.
- **Payment summary:** The *payment summary* is determined by the budget per day and is displayed as estimated monthly costs in the results forecast.

- **Platform-specific elements:** Due to the fact that Microsoft Advertising originates from the Microsoft Group, this advertising platform has a whole range of special features. These include, for example, the possibility to advertise via the XBOX home console environment and for products in the Microsoft Store. Probably the most innovative feature from a marketing perspective is the so-called Key Word Bundle. With just one click, it is possible to book a whole range of different keywords without having to select them individually. A similar automated option also exists for ad copy.

As with Google Ads, buyer personas are also crucial on Microsoft Advertising to ensure that your ads are displayed efficiently. Microsoft Advertising offers a valuable alternative to Google Ads and allows companies to reach their target audience in different ways. By using buyer personas, you can ensure that your ads are tailored to the needs and interests of your customers, regardless of the search engine used. Monitor your campaigns regularly, optimize them continuously, and adjust your strategy to get the best results.

4.5 Outlook

The use of buyer personas for search engine advertising is set to become increasingly crucial in the future. They will continue to be instrumental in how companies comprehend, engage with, and retain their target audiences. Regardless of how the search engine landscape evolves and what technological advancements occur, well-defined and regularly updated buyer personas will remain a vital factor in the success of search advertising. It is therefore essential for companies to invest in further developing their personas to ensure they remain relevant in a rapidly changing digital world.

References

Almukhtar, F., Mahmoodd, N., & Kareem, S. (2021). Search engine optimization: A review. *Applied Computer Science, 17*(1), 70–80.

Bala, M., & Verma, D. (2018). A critical review of digital marketing. *International Journal of Management, IT & Engineering, 8*(10), 321–339.

Bayer, E., Srinivasan, S., Riedl, E. J., & Skiera, B. (2020). The impact of online display advertising and paid search advertising relative to offline advertising on firm performance and firm value. *International Journal of Research in Marketing, 37*(4), 789–804.

Belanche, D., Flavián, C., & Pérez-Rueda, A. (2017). Understanding interactive online advertising: Congruence and product involvement in highly and lowly arousing, skippable video ads. *Journal of Interactive Marketing, 37*(1), 75–88.

Bianchi, T. (2023). *Advertising revenue of Google from 2001 to 2022*. https://www.statista.com/statistics/266249/advertising-revenue-of-google/. Accessed 28 Feb 2023.

Brent, D. (2024). *The Bings ads guide for businesses essential strategies for growing your business with online promotion via Microsoft's advertising platform*. Amazon Digital Services LLC—Kdp.

Chen, M. X., Lee, B. N., Bansal, G., Cao, Y., Zhang, S., Lu, J., et al. (2019). Gmail smart compose: Real-time assisted writing. In *Proceedings of the 25th ACM SIGKDD international conference on knowledge discovery & data mining* (pp. 2287–2295).

Ciepłuch, B., Jacob, R., Mooney, P., & Winstanley, A. C. (2010). Comparison of the accuracy of OpenStreetMap for Ireland with Google maps and Bing maps. In *Proceedings of the ninth international symposium on spatial accuracy assessment in natural resuorces and enviromental*. University of Leicester.

Desai, V., & Vidyapeeth, B. (2019). Digital marketing: A review. *International Journal of Trend in Scientific Research and Development, 5*(5), 196–200.

Ehrlich, H. (2009). Poe in cyberspace: Bing-Microsoft's new search engine and information portal. *The Edgar Allan Poe Review, 10*(3), 126–132.

Halavais, A. (2017). *Search engine society*. Wiley.

Hong, G., Folcarelli, A., Less, J., Wang, C., Erbasi, N., & Lin, S. (2021). Voice assistants and cancer screening: A comparison of Alexa, Siri, Google Assistant, and Cortana. *The Annals of Family Medicine, 19*(5), 447–449.

Islam, M. (2023). *4 things Google should learn from Microsoft Bing*. https://www.linkedin.com/pulse/4-things-google-should-learn-from-microsoft-bing-mirajul-islam/. Accessed 4 Sep 2023.

Jafarzadeh, H., Aurum, A., D'Ambra, J., & Ghapanchi Dr, A. H. (2015). A systematic review on search engine advertising. *Pacific Asia Journal of the Association for Information Systems, 7*(3), 1–32.

Katz, H. (2016). *The media handbook: A complete guide to advertising media selection, planning, research, and buying*. Routledge.

Kelsey, T., & Kelsey, T. (2017). Ad extensions. In *Introduction to search engine marketing and AdWords: A guide for absolute beginners* (pp. 103–113).

Kleindienst, B. (2017). *Performance measurement and management: Design and introduction of performance measurement and control systems*. Springer Gabler.

Langville, A. N., & Meyer, C. D. (2006). *Google's PageRank and beyond: The science of search engine rankings*. Princeton University Press.

Levy, S. (2021). *In the plex: How Google thinks, works, and shapes our lives*. Simon & Schuster.

Li, H., Kannan, P. K., Viswanathan, S., & Pani, A. (2016). Attribution strategies and return on keyword investment in paid search advertising. *Marketing Science, 35*(6), 831–848.

Maddodi, C. B., & Upadhyaya, P. (2024). In-app advertising: A systematic literature review and implications for future research. *Spanish Journal of Marketing-ESIC, 28*(3), 334–355.

Mehta, K., & Singhal, E. (2020). Marketing channel attribution modelling: Markov chain analysis. *International Journal of Indian Culture and Business Management, 21*(1), 63–77.

Mehta, H., Kanani, P., & Lande, P. (2019). Google maps. *International Journal of Computer Applications, 178*(8), 41–46.

Mischke, M. (2023, August 24). *First touch attribution vs last touch: Which one is best?* https://www.whatconverts.com/blog/first-touch-attribution/ Accessed 06 Sep 2023.

Nyagadza, B. (2022). Search engine marketing and social media marketing predictive trends. *Journal of Digital Media & Policy, 13*(3), 407–425.

Pitikaris, H. (2023). *Conversion rate optimization through A/B testing*. https://www.more-fire.com/blog/conversion-rate-optimierung-durch-gezieltes-ab-testing-so-gehts/. Accessed 06 Sep 2023.

Restori, M. (2018). *How to track first-touch attribution in Google analytics*. https://chartio.com/learn/marketing-analytics/how-to-track-first-touch-attribution-in-google-analytics Accessed 06 Sep 2023.

Samuelson, P. (2009). Google book search and the future of books in cyberspace. *Minnesota Law Review, 94*, 1308.

Shewale, R. (2024). *Google search statistics 2024 (most searches & trends)*. https://www.demandsage.com/google-search-statistics/#:~:text=How%20many%20Google%20searches%20per,and%202%20trillion%20searches%20annually. Accessed 19 Aug 2024.

Tavşanoğlu, B. (2018). Decision support system for search engine advertising campaign management by determining negative keywords.

Yang, S., Lin, S., Carlson, J. R., & Ross, W. T., Jr. (2016). Brand engagement on social media: Will firms' social media efforts influence search engine advertising effectiveness? *Journal of Marketing Management, 32*(5–6), 526–557.

5

Display Advertising

What You Will Take Away from This Chapter

- How display advertising has historically evolved into programmatic advertising.
- How programmatic advertising can be used.
- What campaign settings are important in programmatic advertising.

5.1 Characteristics of Display and Programmatic Advertising

5.1.1 Ad Server as the Base Technology for Display Advertising

5.1.1.1 How Ad Servers Work

Display advertising includes all forms of digital advertising that use graphic media such as images and video. Historically, the first and

© The Author(s), under exclusive license to Springer Fachmedien Wiesbaden GmbH, part of Springer Nature 2025
A. Schwarz-Musch et al., *Digital Advertising in the Post-cookie Era*, Business Guides on the Go, https://doi.org/10.1007/978-3-658-47100-2_5

best-known form of display advertising was the banner ad in its various forms and sizes.

But how does display advertising work in the first place?

The basic technology for display advertising is the ad server. They solved many of the problems that existed in the early days of banner advertising. For example, banners had to be manually inserted into the source code of the website by programmers. The downside was that if you had more than 20 subpages, the installation was cumbersome and required specialists. In addition, the inventory on the website became scarce, as campaigns for several advertisers could not be played out according to impressions (=advertisements). In the early 2000s, this often meant that online advertising space could not be sold, resulting in a lack of revenue for the website operator. In addition, the only way to measure success was through log files, which meant that the campaign could only be optimized manually.

Today, ad servers make working in the advertising industry much easier. An ad server works by integrating an ad server tag into the website of the website owner, also known as the publisher. An ad server tag is a short script, i.e., source code, that represents a placeholder for advertising in all advertising formats (image, text, video, sound, etc.). The ad is stored on the ad server and is played and measured when the site is accessed. Today, ad server tags can also be integrated into many other digital touchpoints (Headerbidding.com team, 2022).

5.1.1.2 Ad Server from Publisher and Advertiser Perspective

After installing the ad server tags, a publisher can control, measure, and optimize its clients' ad placements on the touch point. Ad servers also allow many publishers to join together to form an advertising network.

The benefits of using ad servers for publishers include.

- Automated delivery of creative across campaigns.
- Count and automatically optimize ad impressions and clicks/leads.
- Audience targeting.
- Reporting and billing.

Advertisers can also use ad servers. However, this requires specific expertise or personnel and also incurs ad server costs.[1] Technically speaking, the company's own ad server tag is integrated into the publisher's ad server tag. This is called tag-in-tag placement.

As an advertiser, companies can either outsource the use of a central ad server to an agency or operate an ad server themselves. Running your own ad server makes sense if you run many campaigns a year, can build up the necessary expertise in-house, and want to maintain data sovereignty. An ad server is operated via SAS (Software as a Service), i.e., companies do not need any additional hardware and can use the ad server via a simple web browser login.

Using your own ad server, whether through an agency or in-house, offers advertisers a number of advantages:

1. **Centralized reporting across all touchpoints**

   All campaign data from publishers and media is fed into the ad server in real time and can be used in its entirety. If companies use the ad server in-house, they do not have to wait for agency or publisher reports.

2. **Real reach without audience overlap**

   A major benefit of having your own ad server is that you can identify unique users across all touchpoints and control campaigns efficiently by setting a frequency cap.

   Without a centralized ad server, each publisher's ad server counts users only for that publisher and does not recognize audience overlap. In most cases, however, users browse multiple publishers' sites (e.g., news sites) and are counted multiple times as "unique" users due to the lack of a central ad server. As a result, the frequency of exposure is underestimated, resulting in higher advertising costs.

---

[1] Ad servers offer different pricing models based on the number of monthly ad requests and features required. In a comparison of 10 ad servers, the costs for 2, 10, and 25 million ad requests per month were compared. Prices ranged from free (for Revive Ad Server) to $2500/month for 25 million ad requests (for Epom) (Adglare, 2020).

3. Measure and optimize performance during the campaign

A dedicated ad server allows companies to customize campaigns on the fly with a variety of options. Ad media, placements, publishers, frequency caps, visibility, and more can be optimized in real time. Especially if the ad server is operated in-house, this significantly increases the speed of response when optimizing campaigns.

In addition, having your own ad server makes it easier to detect ad fraud,[2] such as irregularities in ad delivery. For example, 1000 clicks on an ad at 4 a.m. with 10,000 ad impressions is easy to spot when only 50 ad impressions with 2 clicks are served at that time on a normal day. It is also easier to identify unwanted ad placements, which can then be corrected immediately.

Having your own ad server also makes it easier to detect ad fraud, such as irregularities in ad delivery. For example, 1000 clicks on an ad at 4 a.m. with 10,000 ad impressions is easy to spot when only 50 ad impressions with 2 clicks are served at that time on a normal day. It is also easier to identify unwanted ad placements, which can then be corrected immediately.

4. Data security and insights

Data security and insights have become increasingly important in the digital marketing landscape in recent years. When companies use an ad server in conjunction with an agency, it is common for the agency, as the operator of the ad server, to access and analyze the campaign data and insights of all its clients. To change this practice, special contracts would have to be negotiated with the agency to establish a separate system for operating the ad server, thereby preventing the agency from collecting and analyzing data. This is both legally and technically challenging. However, in this scenario, the data remains with a third party, the agency.

If the agency changes, campaign data may be lost or access to additional insight data may be unavailable. In contrast, an in-house ad server

---

[2] Ad fraud refers to fraudulent practices that use click fraud or fake impressions to manipulate the billing mechanisms of online advertising campaigns in order to generate financial gain or harm advertisers.

allows for complete control of the data. All current and historical data can be stored internally and used for further analysis or attribution path modeling, ensuring continuous access and sustainable use of data resources.

5. **Customer journey**

With their own ad server, companies can tailor both the campaign and the creative to the different stages of the customer journey. Targeting at the different touch points allows for a consistent and relevant customer approach, which can increase the likelihood of conversions (Malthouse & Li, 2017).

5.1.2 Programmatic Advertising

The technology behind ad servers has continued to evolve, with intelligent algorithms increasingly automating the control of ad server campaigns to increase advertising efficiency. This progressive evolution led to the emergence of programmatic advertising. In recent years, programmatic advertising has overtaken direct bookings (insertion orders) thanks to its automated real-time auction mechanisms for ad placements. By 2022, the global share of programmatic advertising will be around 87% (PwC/IAB, 2023).

Definition "Programmatic advertising describes the automated serving of digital ads in real time based on individual ad impression opportunities" (Busch, 2016).

In simple terms, programmatic advertising means that advertising is no longer purchased manually from publishers, but rather automatically. Negotiations on CPM prices, CPC prices, etc. are no longer carried out by agency staff, but by AI (artificial intelligence). The goal is to achieve the lowest cost-per-thousand (CPM) or cost-per-click (CPC) in the target group to achieve high advertising efficiency. Advertising is purchased

Fig. 5.1 Real-time bidding

in real time during the campaign and is referred to as real-time bidding (RTB).

Real-Time Bidding Real-time bidding (RTB) (Fig. 5.1) is a technology that plays a central role in programmatic advertising. It enables the automated, auction-based purchase of advertising space in real time. RTB allows advertisers to bid for and buy individual impressions in milliseconds as soon as an ad space becomes available. The RTB process optimizes media buying by efficiently managing costs while providing the ability to precisely target audiences.

In this bidding process, the advertiser specifies the maximum CPM at which they are willing to book advertising before the campaign starts. The publisher, on the other hand, specifies the minimum price at which it is willing to sell the ad space. The ad server then decides within milliseconds whether these two factors are met and plays the ad in real time or not. In this example, however, there may not be enough inventory available on the publisher's site at the minimum price offered. If an advertiser does not get a chance, they will have to increase their bid.

To avoid reaching a publisher's inventory limits, there are demand-side and sell-side platforms that can be connected via an ad exchange (Fig. 5.2). On the demand side, many advertisers can place their bids. On the sell-side platform, many publishers submit their bids and the ad exchange automatically matches supply and demand.

But programmatic advertising goes far beyond automated buying and selling, using a variety of technologies to control the automated buying, placement, and selection of ad formats, and campaign optimization of

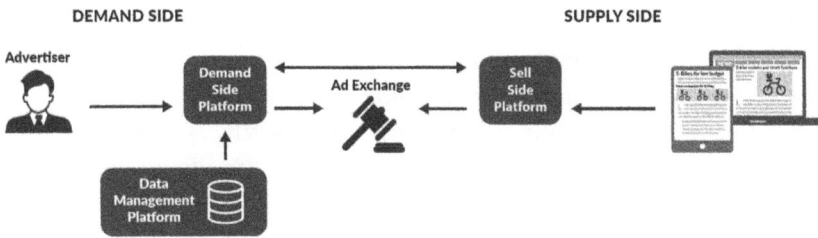

Fig. 5.2 Ad exchange

digital advertising. This minimizes wastage and increases advertising efficiency. The basis for this is user data, which is highly relevant for success. The greater the quantity and quality of the data, the more effective the advertising campaigns (Noller & Magalon, 2016). With data a distinction is made between.

- **First-party data** refers to information that companies collect directly from their own customers or website visitors, such as through CRM or loyalty programs. It includes data such as names, addresses, site interaction details, and purchase history. This data is highly valuable because companies can use it for direct communication and personalization efforts, leveraging their pre-existing relationship with customers.
- **Second-party data** is collected by one organization but shared with another in a mutually beneficial arrangement. For example, if a user searches on one platform and clicks through to an advertiser's site, the search behavior itself is considered second-party data, while actions taken on the advertiser's site (such as viewing or purchasing a product) become first-party data for the advertiser.
- **Third-party data** comes from external sources that are not directly connected to the customer. Typically aggregated and purchased from data brokers, it includes demographic, psychographic, and behavioral information collected across multiple sites and platforms. This data is valuable for targeting broad audiences, especially in cases where first or second party data is not available (Brosche & Kumar, 2016).

The Data Management Platform (DMP) stores, processes, and enhances user data from first, second, and third parties. This data can be stored and processed on the demand side, i.e., the advertiser's side, as well as on the supply side. From the advertiser's perspective, however, only the demand side is usually considered (Brosche & Kumar, 2016; Rask, 2023).

The **Data Management Platform** (DPM) mentioned above plays a key role in programmatic advertising. This is where all relevant user data is collected and managed. It is used to collect, manage, and analyze large amounts of structured and unstructured data from multiple sources. It enables advertisers and agencies to segment and understand audiences more accurately to increase the efficiency of advertising campaigns.

The DMP is characterized by the following features and requirements:

- **Comprehensive data integration**
    The DMP must be able to integrate data from multiple sources, such as online and offline channels, CRM systems, social media, and mobile applications. This requires flexible connectors and data processing capabilities to import and transform data in different formats and structures. Comprehensive integration enables a holistic view of the customer and improves personalization in marketing campaigns.
- **Efficient data organization and segmentation**
    A DMP should be able to effectively organize, categorize, and segment large volumes of data. This requires powerful algorithms and processing capabilities to enable fast and accurate analysis. Efficient data organization is essential for targeted marketing activities, enabling granular audience segmentation.
- **Analytics and reporting**
    Built-in analytics and reporting tools are critical for deriving actionable insights from collected data. This requires statistical models, machine learning algorithms, and visualization tools that enable marketers to make data-driven decisions and optimize campaign performance. Such tools increase the efficiency and accuracy of data analysis and improve the understanding of customer behavior and preferences.
- **Data privacy and compliance**
    With increasing demands for data privacy, a DMP must ensure that data is processed in compliance with regulations such as

GDPR. This includes data anonymization and consent management capabilities to ensure data security and privacy at all times.
- **Scalability and flexibility**

  A DMP must be scalable and flexible to keep pace with business growth and the evolving data landscape. The platform should be able to handle increasing data volumes and respond quickly to new technologies and changing market dynamics.
- **Integration with specific marketing platforms**

  In addition to general requirements, a DMP may offer specific integration options, such as with preferred marketing platforms or tools. This feature enables seamless transitions and synchronization of marketing data and activities, which is especially important for organizations with complex MarTech infrastructures.
- **Advanced analytics capabilities**

  To address specific business needs, the DMP can also support specialized analytics, such as predictive analytics or customer journey mapping. These advanced capabilities help uncover deeper insights from data and enable targeted optimization of marketing strategies (AppsFlyer, n.d.; Lawrence, 2024; Secoda, n.d.; Tikait, 2024).

A thorough assessment of these requirements is critical for organizations to ensure that the DMP meets their specific data and marketing needs and fully realizes its potential to optimize the customer journey and facilitate data-driven decision-making.

A DMP typically processes anonymized third-party data such as IP addresses, device information, and cookies. With the advent of the cookie-less era and the elimination of third-party cookies, third-party data collection is becoming increasingly difficult. As a result, **customer data platforms** (CDPs) are becoming the focus of programmatic advertising. Unlike DMPs, CDPs also integrate first-party data, which is data that comes directly from the customer. This includes email addresses, postal addresses, and phone numbers (Treasure Data, 2024). By integrating first-party data, CDPs enable a more detailed understanding of target audiences and promote the effectiveness of personalized advertising campaigns. The differences between a DPM and a CDP are summarized in Fig. 5.3.

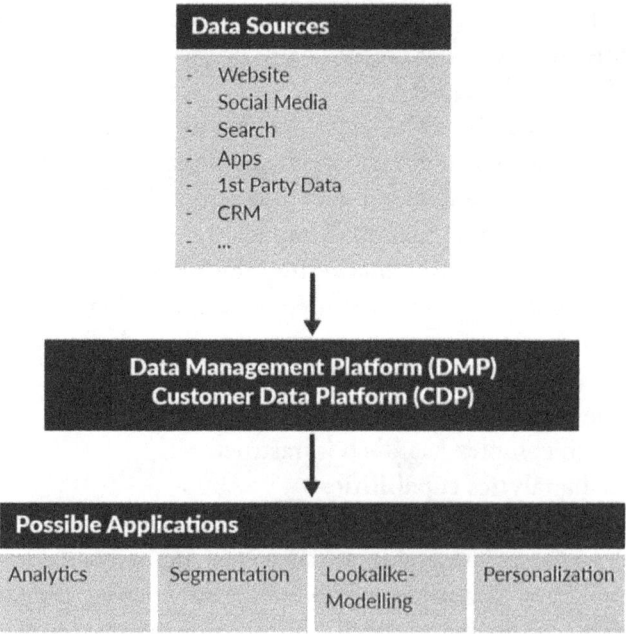

Fig. 5.3 Data management platform

Building on the functions and capabilities of DMPs and CDPs, a **Dynamic Banner Tool** (DBT) can be integrated to dynamically design the advertising content. The term "banner" refers not only to classic image banners, but also to commercials that can be broadcast as videos on television, for example. The DBT uses the data from the DMP to select and play the most appropriate ad based on the user's profile. The interaction of DMP, CDP, and DBT enables targeted and personalized ad delivery across multiple formats and channels.

The following example (Fig. 5.4) illustrates how all these areas work together in programmatic advertising:

Example The furniture store wants to sell its diverse kitchen collection, but the problem is that it covers a wide range of price points, so broad campaigns often result in high waste. To date, monthly flyers with special offers and discounts have been sent to all households in Austria between

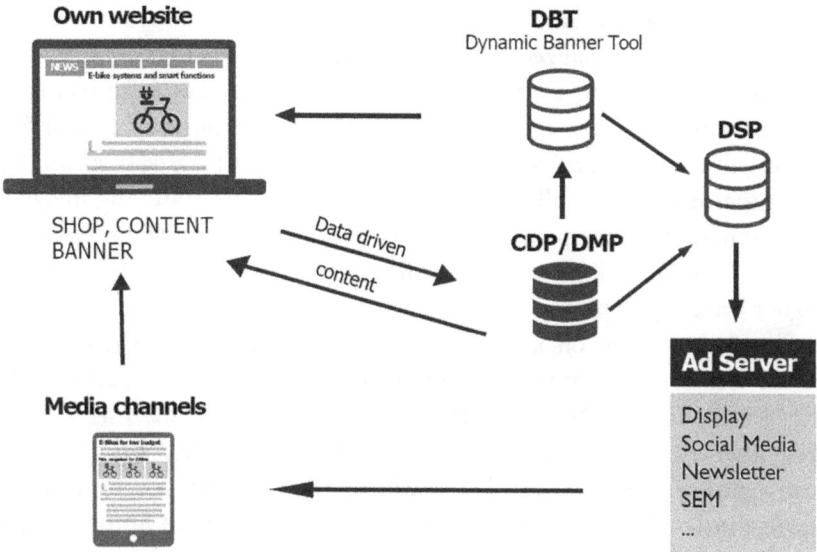

Fig. 5.4 Practical example of programmatic advertising

the ages of 18 and 60. However, operators face the challenge of effectively targeting their different audiences—such as students, young families, singles, and DINKs (Double Income No Kids)—with high-reach campaigns without knowing exactly where these customer segments are in the customer journey. Given the different lifespans of kitchens—around 10 years for an affordable kitchen and 20–30 years for a high-end kitchen—it is unlikely that a household that has recently purchased a kitchen for around €30,000 will need another kitchen in the near future.

To counter this, the furniture store acquires anonymized data from a large real estate website and integrates it into its DMP. The logic behind this: People who search for houses or apartments on real estate sites may be in the process of buying or renting and therefore need a new kitchen. This assumption is based on internal and external market research. By analyzing the property search criteria, such as price range, square footage, or location, the furniture store can estimate the household income and make appropriate kitchen offers.

The following campaign uses a demand-side platform (DSP) to launch a high-reach campaign. The user groups identified on the real estate site are targeted in advertising networks. The Dynamic Banner Tool (DBT) is used to create personalized and automated ad banners that are displayed in real time based on estimated household income. For example, users who have searched for a 45 sqm apartment with a monthly cost of 500 euros will receive an offer for an affordable kitchen for 1490 euros. The ad banner is automatically created in the DBT with a matching image of the kitchen and the special price. Users looking for a 200m^2 house in Vienna Döbling will be presented with a Designer Edition kitchen in the higher price segment.

When these users click on the ad, they are redirected to the furniture store's website. The content of the website automatically adapts to the user profile in the DMP. The landing page with the matching kitchen and other kitchen accessories is also displayed when the website is visited again via retargeting. The user's interactions on the website are incorporated into the user profile in the DMP, which improves the assessment of the user's customer journey stage and can be adjusted in the DMP.

The next step is to further classify the user profiles and launch an additional campaign using lookalike modeling. This involves identifying similar user profiles in ad networks and DSPs in order to serve ads to users with similar profile characteristics. The assumption is that digital twins with similar profiles will have similar buying characteristics. This assumption may or may not be true. The match rate of the profiles affects the reach of the campaign: reducing the match rate from 100% to 90%, for example, can increase the reach. Real-time performance measurement is critical to evaluate the effectiveness of lookalike modeling and make adjustments to best achieve campaign goals.

Depending on the stage of the customer journey, the furniture store can move users from one stage to the next—and ultimately to the purchase stage and the goal of "buying a kitchen."

Programmatic TV advertising is experiencing strong growth, driven by the rise of connected TVs (CTV), the shift away from traditional linear TV, and the increasing availability of data for targeting purposes. Key benefits for advertisers include more precise targeting, enhanced efficiency and measurability, and greater scalability (Grapeseed Media, 2022; IncrementX, 2024; SmartHub, 2024).

5.2 Campaign Settings

5.2.1 Goals, Performance Measurement, and Optimization

With programmatic advertising, companies can reach their customers throughout the entire customer journey, from purchase to repurchase, and automatically optimize their conversions.

Programmatic advertising offers companies many opportunities for **automated performance measurement and optimization**. A critical first step is for companies to be clear about their goals. Measurable key performance indicators (KPIs) can then be defined for these goals and then automatically optimized.

Unlike popular platforms such as Facebook, Instagram, YouTube, or Google, where the targets to be optimized are selected at the beginning of the campaign creation process, programmatic advertising requires **individual target definition** on the part of the advertising company. In consultation with agencies or publishers, it must be determined which KPIs are technically measurable and can therefore be optimized, and whether a suitable billing model can be implemented. The advantage of programmatic advertising is that it is much more flexible than the platforms mentioned above and offers a wider range of options for measuring success and optimization (Davis, 2023).

A key benefit of programmatic advertising is the ability to automate billing based on goal achievement. This means that advertising is billed on the basis of defined KPIs such as products sold, clicks, app installs, unique users, impressions, newsletter registrations, brochure pages viewed, or test drives for car brands (Befoundonline, 2022).

Here it becomes clear that all the "big goals" that companies want to achieve in the course of a customer journey can be measured, optimized, and billed programmatically using KPIs. These can be found, for example, in the.

- **Awareness phase**: Create awareness, drive traffic to touchpoints (KPIs such as impressions, clicks…)
- **Consideration (Ask) phase**: generate interest through interactions (KPIs: likes, comments, etc.), clicks, leads (app installs, newsletter subscriptions, downloads…)
- **Buy (Act) phase**: completion of the purchase (KPIs: revenue, sales…)

In addition to the top KPIs (Sect. 2.4), other metrics can be used, e.g., metrics that can be used to evaluate the efficiency of actions (e.g., cost per impression, cost per click, cost per lead, cost per sale). In addition, metrics such as visibility can also be measured and optimized. In the case of viewability, only impressions that were displayed for more than 2 s and where at least 80% of the content was visible are taken into account.

5.2.2 Targeting and Booking Options

There are many targeting options available in programmatic advertising that allow advertising campaigns to be precisely targeted. Examples of common targeting options include demographic, geographic or behavioral targeting, as well as contextual targeting or retargeting (Grapeseed Media, 2022; SmartHub, 2024). These options can be combined to target campaigns to specific user groups. Technically, this combination is implemented using specialized programmatic advertising platforms and tools that allow for fine-grained targeting of campaign.

When using different targeting options, it is important to strike a balance so that you do not overly limit your reach. Overly restricting the reach by combining too many targeting options can significantly reduce the overall reach of the campaign and thus the effectiveness of the advertising campaign.

Another important aspect is ongoing monitoring and performance evaluation, as targeting relies on technical systems and data that may not always deliver the expected results. Regular analysis and adjustments can improve targeting strategies and ensure campaign effectiveness. Best practices and lessons learned from past campaigns can provide valuable guidance.

The following example shows how targeting can work in the case of a delivery service:

Example A food delivery service uses programmatic advertising and defines various targeting criteria for its ad campaign to target potential customers. The defined targeting options include weather targeting, geo-targeting, and time-based targeting.

The programmatic advertising platform used by the delivery service is programmed to access the weather forecast and activate weather targeting when rain is forecast. Combined with geo-targeting, the advertising is focused on the areas where rain is expected.

On the evening in question, after the office closes at around 4 p.m., the platform uses time targeting to place ads on social media. The ad suggests spending the rainy evening with a romantic movie and a delivery order. The selection of the romantic movie is based on the interest targeting of the social media user's profile. The person who sees the ad on social media takes the subway and continues to surf the web. When they get off the train, they pass digital posters that use geo-targeting and retargeting to recognize that the person is passing by and has already seen the first ad.

The user profile shows that the person likes Asian food. An ad for the delivery service quickly appears on the digital billboard, now advertising Asian food for a cozy movie night on a rainy day. The ad suggests ordering now for the movie night so that the food will be delivered on time at 8:15 pm.

If the person has not ordered yet, the ad is shown again during the first commercial break on the smart TV, encouraging them to order their favorite food. These TV ads are personalized and delivered based on favorite food, supported by renewed geo-targeting and interest targeting.

The coordinated use of these targeting options enables the delivery service to run a personalized and relevant advertising campaign across multiple channels and platforms, effectively drawing the attention of the target audience to the offer.

5.2.3 Quality Criteria

In programmatic advertising, the quality and effectiveness of online advertising campaigns also depend heavily on the settings made in advance. The following criteria are key.

1. **Frequency cap**

Programmatic advertising and ad servers can be used to implement a frequency cap across all connected touchpoints, including digital TV and radio channels, as well as other digital and programmatic touchpoints. It is important to ensure that all paid touchpoints are measured in order to set the frequency cap correctly. Otherwise, the exact overlap of users and frequency cap compliance is often guesswork when advertising is served across multiple ad networks.

Traditionally, frequency capping has relied on third-party cookies, but their use is declining as we move into a cookie-less era. New technical solutions are now being developed to address this challenge and enable effective frequency capping in a cookie-free world (Johnson et al., 2022). These include well-known solutions such as contextual targeting and identity solutions. Identity solutions aim to recognize users across platforms and devices, even in the absence of cookies. Some of the approaches include using email hashes, device IDs, and other pseudonymized identifiers to track and recognize users.

2. **Brand safety**

Brand safety is an essential component of programmatic advertising, as the automated nature of these ad bookings can make it easy to lose track of which sites the ads are appearing on. There have been cases in the past where programmatic advertising has inadvertently displayed ads in a racist or sexual context, which has had a negative impact on brand image (Johnson et al., 2023).

To ensure a safe brand environment, there are several mechanisms and tools available in programmatic advertising. These include **whitelists**, which allow only verified and safe sites to display ads, and **blacklists**, which exclude potentially harmful or inappropriate sites. Filters can also be used to block specific categories of content.

Specialized **brand safety tools** such as Double Verify are also useful tools. They crawl the web, analyze, categorize, and semantically evaluate content to block ads from appearing on certain sites. These brand safety tools should be an integral part of programmatic advertising campaign management and actively used to protect brand integrity and ensure that ads are served in an appropriate and safe environment (Carah & Brodmerkel, 2022).

3. **Ad fraud**

Programmatic advertising campaigns tend to have a higher rate of ad fraud than traditional digital advertising campaigns. It is therefore essential that programmatic platform providers adhere to strict security standards and continually work to improve these standards. Advertisers should be aware of the risks of ad fraud and take appropriate measures to protect themselves.

Ad fraud often occurs at touchpoints, particularly on sites where advertisers have limited control. The type of fraudulent activity can vary depending on the billing model, and may include fake impressions, fake leads, and similar fraudulent activity. These fraud attempts are designed to increase costs for advertisers without delivering real value or engagement (Sadeghpour & Vlajic, 2021).

In addition to relying on the security protocols of programmatic platforms, it is advisable to implement your own monitoring and control measures. This could include reviewing performance metrics, working with trusted and transparent partners, and using fraud prevention technologies to ensure that ad dollars are being spent effectively and that campaigns are reaching the desired audience.

The following measures can be taken to ensure the integrity of any programmatic advertising campaign:

- It is a good idea to ask programmatic platform and real-time bidding vendors to provide any anti-fraud precautions they have in place, including the associated certificates. One way to verify vendors could be through the Tag Today platform.
- Limit your whitelisting[3] to premium vendors and use ad verification providers[4] such as Integral Ad Science, Confiant or Meetrics Adjust to verify the quality of ad impressions (Wlosik, 2024).
- A performance-optimized KPI, including a billing model that only charges for successful purchases in your store, can be useful. Verified purchases in your online store are not very attractive to fraudsters. However, this model is only appropriate for campaigns with a "sales" goal.
- You or your agency should monitor the campaign for anomalies, such as unusually high click-through rates, impressions, or increased traffic from distant countries at suspicious times. The duration of ad impressions can also be misleading. For example, if ads are only shown for 1 s on average, or if there are only machine views instead of human interactions. A bot can easily do this and even falsify the viewability rate by scrolling.
- Domain spoofing is a popular fraud technique that targets programmatic campaigns. It involves the fraudster redirecting traffic to an illegitimate domain that looks like a legitimate domain. Some fraudsters even go so far as to recreate trusted websites. Organizations should randomly test touchpoints. Legitimate touchpoints have an imprint and are listed in trustworthy advertising lists (e.g., at oewa.at). If this information is missing, it could be a traffic generation platform that only generates machine-generated traffic.
- One recommendation is to use ad fraud solutions that detect ad fraud during the campaign, not after. Automated systems can measure

---

[3] Whitelisting refers to the selection of trustworthy publishers.
[4] Adverification checks whether the ad is displayed by the user in the right context, environment and correct placement on a website for example.

anomalies and sound the alarm. These irregularities can occur not only on websites, but across all programmatic touchpoints (Wakefield & Mussard, 2020).

4. Visibility

In programmatic advertising, viewability tracking allows you to effectively measure and track the viewability of ads across a wide range of ad formats. This includes text, image, and video ads, where it is possible to track exactly how much of the ad was viewed and for how long, on average. This can be broken down into different time periods for a more granular view. The average alone can sometimes be misleading. A more detailed analysis of the percentage of users who watched the ad for less than a second or watched it to the end provides more insight. This information can be used to optimize the ad for the next campaign. It is also possible to test during the campaign and intervene if necessary (Next Millennium Media, n.d.; Expósito-Ventura et al., 2016; Uhl et al., 2020).

References

Adglare. (2020, September 18). *Pricing: Quick comparison of 10 ad servers*. Adglare Ad Service Software. Retrieved from https://www.adglare.com/pricing-quick-comparison-of-10-ad-servers-2020-67336

AppsFlyer. (n.d.). *Data management platform (DMP)*. Retrieved October 11, 2024, from https://www.appsflyer.com/glossary/data-management-platform/

Befoundonline. (2022). *7 programmatic ad KPIs to measure digital campaign success*. Retrieved from https://befoundonline.com/blog/7-programmatic-ad-kpis-to-measure-success/

Brosche, K., & Kumar, A. (2016). Realtime data accelerates online marketing. In O. Busch (Ed.), *Programmatic advertising*. Springer. https://doi.org/10.1007/978-3-319-25023-6_18

Busch, O. (2016). The programmatic advertising principle. In O. Busch (Ed.), *Programmatic advertising*. Springer. https://doi.org/10.1007/978-3-319-25023-6_1

Carah, N., & Brodmerkel, S. (2022). *From brand safety to suitability: Advertisers in platform governance.* Internet Policy Review. Retrieved from https://policyreview.info/articles/analysis/safety-to-suitability-advertisers-in-platform-governance

Davis, S. (2023). *Key KPIs for full-funnel programmatic advertising.* Retrieved from https://roirevolution.com/blog/key-kpis-for-full-funnel-programmatic-advertising/

Expósito-Ventura, M., Zhang, H., & Miller, K. (2016). Viewable impressions: Challenges and advancements in measurement and application in programmatic advertising. *IEEE Access, 4,* 307–318. https://doi.org/10.1109/ACCESS.2016

Grapeseed Media. (2022, August 30). *The evolution of programmatic TV ads.* Written by Mason Widmer. Retrieved from https://grapeseedmedia.com/blog/programmatic-tv-ads/

Headerbidding.com Team. (2022). *What is an ad tag?* Retrieved from https://headerbidding.com/programmatic-101/what-is-an-ad-tag/

IncrementX. (2024). *The rise of programmatic CTV: What to expect in 2024.* Retrieved from https://www.incrementx.com/blog/the-rise-of-programmatic-ctv-what-to-expect-in-2024/

Johnson, G., Runge, J., & Seufert, E. (2022). Privacy-centric digital advertising: Implications for research. *Customer Needs and Solutions, 9*(1), 49–54. https://doi.org/10.1007/s40547-022-00125-4

Johnson, R., Voorhees, C. M., & Khodakarami, F. (2023). Is your brand protected? *Journal of Advertising Research, 63,* 205–220.

Lawrence, H. (2024, February). *The role of data management platforms in digital marketing.* Inline Insight. Retrieved from https://www.inlineinsight.com/blog/the-impact-of-digital-marketing-0

Malthouse, E. C., & Li, H. (2017). Personalized digital advertising: How data-driven strategies are shaping the future of marketing. *Journal of Advertising Research, 57*(4), 356–361.

Noller, S., & Magalon, F. (2016). Programmatic brand advertising. In O. Busch (Ed.), *Programmatic advertising.* Springer. https://doi.org/10.1007/978-3-319-25023-6_9

PwC & IAB. (2023). *Internet advertising report: Full year 2022.* Retrieved from https://www.iab.com/insights/internet-advertising-revenue-report-full-year-2022/

Rask, O. (2023). *What is programmatic advertising? Everything you need to know*. Retrieved from https://www.match2one.com/blog/what-is-programmatic-advertising/

Sadeghpour, S., & Vlajic, N. (2021). Ads and fraud: A comprehensive survey of fraud in online advertising. *Journal of Cybersecurity and Privacy, 1*(4), 804–832. https://doi.org/10.3390/jcp1040039

Secoda. (n.d.). *What is a data management platform (DMP)?* Retrieved October 11, 2024, from https://www.secoda.co/glossary/what-is-a-data-management-platform-dmp

SmartHub. (2024, April 29). *12 top programmatic advertising trends in 2024*. Written by Roman Vrublivskyi. Retrieved from https://smart-hub.io/blog/top-programmatic-advertising-trends-for-2024/

Tikait, P. (2024, August 15). *What is a data management platform (DMP)? The comprehensive guide. SelectHub*. Retrieved from https://www.selecthub.com/business-intelligence/data-management-platform/

Treasure Data. (2024, May 23). *CDP vs. DMP: What's the difference?* https://www.treasuredata.com/learn/cdp-vs-dmp/

Uhl, C., Nabout, N. A., & Miller, K. (2020). How much ad viewability is enough? The effect of display ad viewability on advertising effectiveness. arXiv preprint, arXiv:2008.12132. Retrieved from https://arxiv.org/abs/2008.12132

Wakefield, L., & Mussard, H. (2020). *The IAB-Europe guide to ad fraud*. Retrieved from https://iabeurope.eu/wp-content/uploads/2020/12/IAB-Europe-Guide-to-Ad-Fraud.pdf

Wlosik, M. (2024, April 26). *What is ad verification and how does it work? Clearcode*. Retrieved from https://clearcode.cc/blog/ad-verification/

GPSR Compliance

The European Union's (EU) General Product Safety Regulation (GPSR) is a set of rules that requires consumer products to be safe and our obligations to ensure this.

If you have any concerns about our products, you can contact us on

ProductSafety@springernature.com

In case Publisher is established outside the EU, the EU authorized representative is:

Springer Nature Customer Service Center GmbH
Europaplatz 3
69115 Heidelberg, Germany

www.ingramcontent.com/pod-product-compliance
Lightning Source LLC
LaVergne TN
LVHW041204250326
834689LV00001BA/8